INTEGRATING MICROSOFT® OFFICE VERSION 4.2/4.3

Sarah E. Hutchinson
Glen J. Coulthard

With Special Thanks To
Doug MacPherson

THE IRWIN ADVANTAGE SERIES
FOR COMPUTER EDUCATION
◆
IRWIN

Chicago • Bogota • Boston • Buenos Aires • Caracas
London • Madrid • Mexico City • Sydney • Toronto

Printed in the United States of America.

ISBN 0-256-18921-8

Microsoft is a registered trademark of Microsoft Corporation.

1 2 3 4 5 6 7 8 9 0 ML 1 0 9 8 7 6 5 4

TABLE OF CONTENTS

SESSION 1: FUNDAMENTALS

SESSION 2: SHARING INFORMATION

SESSION 3: WORKING WITH OBJECTS

SESSION 4: STEP-BY-STEP WITH OLE

SESSION 5: APPLYING WHAT YOU KNOW

USING THIS GUIDE

This tutorial is one in a series of learning guides that lead you through the most popular microcomputer software programs available. Concepts, skills, and procedures are grouped into session topics and are presented in a logical and structured manner. Commands and procedures are introduced using hands-on examples, and you are encouraged to perform the steps along with the guide. Although you may turn directly to a later session, be aware that some sessions require, or at least assume, that you have completed the previous sessions. For maximum benefit, you should also work through the short answer questions and hands-on exercises appearing at the end of each session.

The exercises and examples in this guide use several standard conventions to indicate menu options, keystroke combinations, and command instructions.

MENU INSTRUCTIONS

In Windows, all Menu bar options and pull-down menu commands have an underlined or highlighted letter in each option. When you need to execute a command from the Menu bar—the row of menu choices across the top of the screen—the tutorial's instruction line separates the Menu bar option from the command with a comma. For example, the command for quitting Windows is shown as:

CHOOSE: File, Exit

This instruction tells you to choose the File option on the Menu bar and then to choose the Exit command from the File pull-down menu. The actual steps for choosing a menu command are discussed later in this guide.

KEYSTROKES AND KEYSTROKE COMBINATIONS

When two keys must be pressed together, the tutorial's instruction line shows the keys joined with a plus (+) sign. For example, you can execute a command from the Windows Menu bar by holding down **Alt** and then pressing the key with the underlined or highlighted letter of the desired command.

To illustrate this type of keystroke combination, the following statement shows how to access the File menu option:

PRESS: Alt+f

In this instruction, you press the Alt key first and hold it down while you press f. Once both keys have been pressed, they are then immediately released.

COMMAND INSTRUCTIONS

This guide indicates with a special typeface data that you are required to type in yourself. For example:

TYPE: Income Statement

When you are required to enter unique information, such as the current date or your name, the instruction appears in italics. The following instruction directs you to type your name in place of the actual words: "your name."

TYPE: *your name*

Instructions that use general directions rather than a specific option or command name appear italicized in the regular typeface.

SELECT: *a different pattern for the chart*

ADVANTAGE DISKETTE

The Advantage Diskette, provided with this guide or by your instructor, contains the files that you use in each session and in the hands-on exercises. This diskette is extremely important for ensuring the success of the guide.

If you are using this guide in a self-study program, we suggest that you make a copy of the Advantage Diskette using the DOS DISKCOPY command. When the guide asks you to insert the Advantage Diskette, you insert and work with the copied diskette instead. By following this procedure, you will be able to work through the guide again at a later date using a fresh copy of the Advantage Diskette. For more information on using the DISKCOPY command, please refer to your DOS manual.

HARDWARE ASSUMPTIONS

To run Microsoft Office 4.2 Standard Edition or Microsoft Office 4.3 Professional Edition, you require an 80386- or 80486-based computer with Microsoft Windows 3.1 or later. A VGA or better monitor is also required. In addition, we strongly recommend that your system have a mouse and at least 8 MB of RAM to complete the exercises in this guide.

SOFTWARE ASSUMPTIONS

To successfully complete the exercises in this guide, you must install a complete version of Office on your system, including all of the mini-apps. The mini-apps covered in this guide include: ClipArt Gallery 1.0, Equation Editor 2.0, Graph 5.0, Organization Chart 1.0, and WordArt 2.0. In addition, you must also have Microsoft Query 1.0.

PRIOR LEARNING ASSUMPTIONS

This guide contains intermediate-level material. It is important to your success that you complete the Microsoft Word 6.0 for Windows and Microsoft Excel 5.0 for Windows student guides before embarking on this guide. Of secondary importance, you should also complete the Microsoft Access 2.0 for Windows and Microsoft PowerPoint 4.0 for Windows student guides. Enjoy your journey through these spectacular products!

INTEGRATING MICROSOFT OFFICE VERSION 4.2/4.3: FUNDAMENTALS

For the price of a single software program only a few years ago, you can now purchase a complete assortment of the hottest new programs available. Microsoft Office 4.2 Standard Edition and Microsoft Office 4.3 Professional Edition provide the most powerful Windows applications ever assembled into one box. This session describes these applications and shows you how Microsoft pulled them together into a cohesive package that can boost your productivity.

PREVIEW

When you have completed this session, you will be able to:

Describe the components of Microsoft Office.

•

Manage multiple applications loaded into memory.

•

Organize your desktop.

•

Customize the Microsoft Office Manager.

•

Access help for integrating the applications provided in Microsoft Office.

Why This Session Is Important
Introducing Microsoft Office
     Installing Office
     Microsoft Word
     Microsoft Excel
     Microsoft PowerPoint
     Microsoft Access
     Microsoft Mail
     Microsoft Mini-Apps
Working with Microsoft Office
     Consistency
     Integration
          Microsoft Office Manager (MOM)
          Microsoft OfficeLinks
          OLE 2.0 Technology
Working with Multiple Applications
     Multitasking
     Organizing Your Desktop
Getting to Know Your MOM
     Using MOM
     Customizing MOM
Getting Help
Summary
     Command Summary
Key Terms
Exercises
     Short Answer
     Hands-On

WHY THIS SESSION IS IMPORTANT

In 1991, an IBM executive stated in a keynote address to software developers that the top four applications for personal computers were word processing and spreadsheets, and word processing and spreadsheets. At that time, WordPerfect and Lotus still owned a majority of the application software market for desktop personal computers and Microsoft was just beginning to make inroads with Windows 3.0. Since most people used only one or two applications, integration and consistency among applications were not major issues. If your peers discovered you using three or more applications, you were immediately labeled a computer guru and given pocket protectors on your birthday!

Today, life is not so simple. Computer users typically require three or four applications to perform their daily work. As a result, issues like integration and consistency have become increasingly important. Applications that provide seamless integration allow users to concentrate on their tasks and worry less about the format in which their data is stored. Consistency among applications determines how quickly users can become productive with new applications. The increasing popularity of integrated programs and application software **suites** or **offices** may be attributable to users who now demand that their applications look the same, work seamlessly together, and share information graciously. And it doesn't end there—they also want these tools and features for a fraction of the cost of purchasing the applications separately.

Several of the major software companies are meeting market demand by creating, or at least contributing to, software suites or offices. The differences between individual off-the-shelf applications and their siblings in suites or offices are often negligible, if any. Most companies, such as Microsoft, Lotus, and WordPerfect/Borland/Novell, simply bundle existing applications with a small program that acts as a control center. The control center provides an efficient means for launching and switching among the primary applications—Microsoft Office has MOM (Microsoft Office Manager), Lotus SmartSuite has the SmartCenter, and WordPerfect/Borland/Novell has DAD (Desktop Application Director).

In this session, you are introduced to the component applications that make up Microsoft Office. You learn how to work efficiently with multiple application programs, use the Windows Task Manager and the Microsoft Office Manager, and access the Microsoft Office Help facility.

INTRODUCING MICROSOFT OFFICE

Microsoft Office is produced by Microsoft Corporation, the developers of MS-DOS and Microsoft Windows. There are two versions of Microsoft Office for Windows that are currently available: Microsoft Office 4.2 Standard Edition and Microsoft Office 4.3 Professional Edition. The Standard Edition contains the following applications:

- Microsoft Word 6.0 for Windows
- Microsoft Excel 5.0 for Windows
- Microsoft PowerPoint 4.0 for Windows and a
- Microsoft Mail workstation license for network users.

The Professional Edition adds Microsoft Access 2.0 for Windows to the bundle. These applications are packaged into a single box for a fraction of the combined cost you would pay for each product separately. Microsoft Office is also available for the Macintosh and PowerPC platforms.

INSTALLING MICROSOFT OFFICE

The Microsoft Office installation program copies the desired applications, along with several smaller applications called **mini-apps**, to your hard disk. (*Note*: If your computer has a CD ROM drive, you can install Office using a CD ROM instead of swapping over 20 diskettes into the diskette drive.) For Office Professional, you require a 386 or better computer with 29 MB of free hard disk space for a minimum installation and 82 MB for a complete installation. Once installed, you will require at least 6 MB of RAM (random access memory) to execute the applications. We strongly recommend a 486 or better computer with a minimum of 8 MB of RAM if you will be using two or more applications simultaneously.

A typical installation of Office Professional creates directory folders under the \MSOFFICE directory and the \WINDOWS\MSAPPS directory. (*Note*: You specify the desired directories for each application during the installation process. Therefore, the following example may differ from the directory structure appearing on your computer.) In addition to the folders shown on the next page, there are several subdirectory folders created under each of the main application folders: Word, Excel, PowerPoint, and Access. These subdirectory folders contain samples, templates, and other application-specific files.

Table 1.1

Sample Microsoft
Office Directory
Structure.

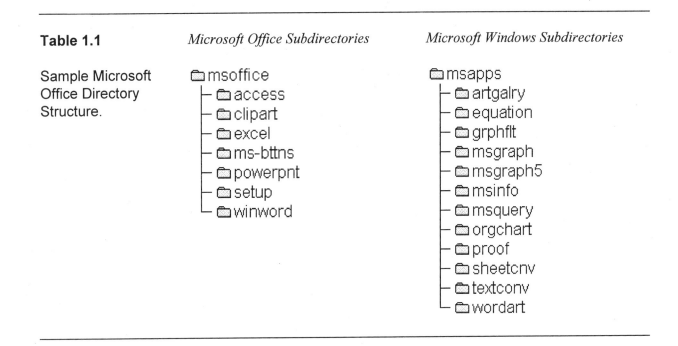

Microsoft Office Subdirectories

```
📁 msoffice
├─ 📁 access
├─ 📁 clipart
├─ 📁 excel
├─ 📁 ms-bttns
├─ 📁 powerpnt
├─ 📁 setup
└─ 📁 winword
```

Microsoft Windows Subdirectories

```
📁 msapps
├─ 📁 artgalry
├─ 📁 equation
├─ 📁 grphflt
├─ 📁 msgraph
├─ 📁 msgraph5
├─ 📁 msinfo
├─ 📁 msquery
├─ 📁 orgchart
├─ 📁 proof
├─ 📁 sheetcnv
├─ 📁 textconv
└─ 📁 wordart
```

Let's take a brief tour of the primary applications in Microsoft Office.

MICROSOFT WORD

Microsoft Word 6.0 for Windows is a word processing software program that lets you create, edit, format, print, and permanently store documents, such as letters, memos, and reports. In addition to the standard word processing capabilities, Word 6.0 provides the following features:

- normal, page layout, and outline views
- wizards and templates for creating tables, performing mail merges, and writing standard documents such as agendas and resumes
- multi-page print preview for showing and editing multiple pages on-screen at the same time
- special "Auto" features like AutoCorrect, AutoText, AutoFormat, and AutoCaption

MICROSOFT EXCEL

Microsoft Excel 5.0 for Windows is an electronic spreadsheet for organizing, analyzing, and charting statistical, financial, and mathematical data. Some of Excel's key features include the following:

- workbooks that may contain worksheets, chart sheets, macro sheets, and Visual Basic programming modules
- spreadsheet publishing with fonts, borders, colors, and patterns
- wizards for entering functions, importing text files, creating crosstab tables, and charting worksheet data
- special "Auto" features like AutoFill and AutoFormat

MICROSOFT POWERPOINT

Microsoft PowerPoint 4.0 for Windows is a presentation graphics program that enables you to create on-screen presentations, overhead transparencies, speaker's notes, audience handouts, and 35mm slides. In addition to hundreds of predefined templates for slide backgrounds, PowerPoint provides the following features:

- ability to insert text, clip art, graphics, charts, and other types of media
- special transitional effects and time-coding options
- wizards for creating slides, recommending content, and picking styles and colors for presentations
- special "Auto" features like AutoContent and AutoLayout

MICROSOFT ACCESS

Available in Office 4.3 Professional Edition, Microsoft Access 2.0 for Windows is a relational database management system for microcomputers. Access enables you to store and manipulate large amounts of data. For example, you can use Access to maintain inventory records, sort personnel lists, and summarize accounting data. Some key features include the following:

- ability to store millions of records in databases up to 1 GB in size
- graphical query-by-example (QBE) for performing complex search and retrieval operations
- wizards for creating forms, reports, and mailing labels
- Cue Cards that provide step-by-step, on-screen help at all times

MICROSOFT MAIL

Microsoft Office also provides a workstation license for Microsoft Mail for Windows. To use Mail, you need to be connected to a network with Microsoft Mail for PC Networks loaded on the server. The Mail for PC Networks software must be purchased separately from Office. Some of Mail's features include the following:

- send and receive electronic mail with attached files
- ability to route documents to a **workgroup** directly from within an application
- store incoming and outgoing messages and faxes in file folders
- communicate with users on other services, such as the Internet

For further information on using Mail, contact the network administrator or system manager at your school or workplace.

MICROSOFT MINI-APPS

Rather than building similar features into each application, Microsoft makes several mini-apps accessible to all applications. These mini-apps include the following:

ClipArt Gallery   Enables you to select and insert clip art from a library of cataloged images. For example:

Equation Editor   Enables you to create complex equations using special math symbols and typesetting standards. For example:

$$\sigma^2 = \frac{\sum_{i=1}^{N}\left(X_i - \mu\right)^2}{N}$$

Graph   Enables you to easily insert a graph into your document, without having to launch Excel. For example:

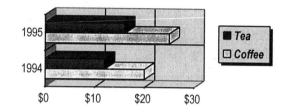

Organization Chart   Enables you to design, build, and insert an organizational chart into your document. For example:

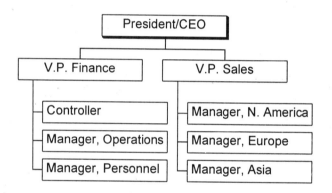

WordArt   Allows you to apply special effects to textual information in your document.

In Session 2, you will use several of these mini-apps in preparing documents, worksheets, and slides.

WORKING WITH MICROSOFT OFFICE

What do today's sophisticated computer users really want? Among the most common responses: they want their applications to look the same and they want them to work together. This section shows you how Microsoft tackles these issues of consistency and integration in Office.

CONSISTENCY

Consistency among applications is becoming increasingly important. A few years ago, people could focus their attention on one or two applications (for example, WordPerfect or Lotus.) Today, the average number of applications people use on a daily basis has doubled to three or four. The underlying issue, however, is not the number of applications people use, but rather the ease and speed with which they can learn them. If each application's interface differs significantly from the next, you must learn each program from scratch. On the contrary, if the interface among applications is similar, the time spent learning the software is significantly reduced.

To promote consistency within the Office family, all applications share common menus, dialog boxes, toolbar buttons, keyboard shortcuts, and mini-apps. Figure 1.1 illustrates how the top-level menus in Word, Excel, and PowerPoint are identical except for a single application-specific menu command. After working with these three applications, you will also notice that each program has two visible toolbars by default, named *Standard* and *Formatting*. Many of the buttons or icons on these toolbars are available in all Office applications.

Another Office feature implemented to improve consistency is the use of keyboard shortcuts, sometimes called **accelerator keys**. For example, you can press `Ctrl`+s in any Office application to save the current document and `Ctrl`+p to send it to the printer. After learning to perform these keyboard shortcuts in Word, you already know how to save and print a worksheet in Excel.

Figure 1.1

Top-level Menu bars in Microsoft Office's primary applications.

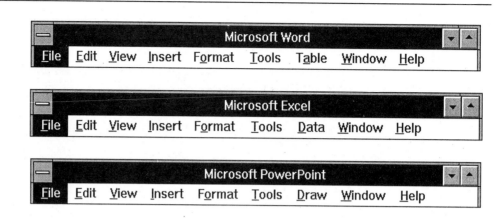

The result of keeping the interface consistent is an extraordinary boost in your productivity and a flattening of your learning curve.

INTEGRATION

If you've ever tried to place a range from a Lotus 1-2-3 worksheet into a WordPerfect 5.1 document, you'll understand the difficulties of integration. Integration refers to your ability to work with multiple applications efficiently and to share information among them. Most software tools are designed for specific tasks, such as formatting text or calculating numerical tables. Unfortunately, we're often tempted to continue working in an application for the sake of simplicity, even though we know it's the wrong tool for the job. For example, how many of us have used a spreadsheet as a word processor because we needed a table and a chart on the same page as some text? Now there's a better and more efficient way to work with multiple applications. In this section, you are introduced to Microsoft Office's integration features: the Microsoft Office Manager (MOM), Microsoft OfficeLinks, and OLE 2.0 technology.

MICROSOFT OFFICE MANAGER (MOM)   The Microsoft Office Manager (MOM) is a small application program that serves as a "control center," "launch pad," or "home base" for the individual Office applications. One of MOM's more useful features is an online Help facility for solving cross-application problems. You can also customize MOM's toolbar by adding icons from other programs (and they don't even have to be Microsoft applications!) Lastly, MOM provides access to the integrated setup and uninstall program for all Office components. Later this session, you will learn how to launch applications and customize MOM.

MICROSOFT OFFICELINKS   Microsoft **OfficeLinks** is a generic term for the means and processes by which the various applications in Microsoft Office are integrated. At the heart of OfficeLinks is OLE 2.0 technology. Two examples of OfficeLinks are the PresentIt (⊞) and ReportIt (⊞) toolbar buttons in Word and PowerPoint. To create a PowerPoint slide presentation from a Word outline, you simply click the PresentIt button (⊞) on the toolbar. To create a Word outline from a slide presentation, you click the ReportIt button (⊞) on the PowerPoint toolbar. There are no other steps involved in the transformation, other than sitting back and watching Microsoft Office and its OfficeLinks go to work.

OLE 2.0 TECHNOLOGY   Microsoft's **Object Linking and Embedding (OLE)** technology lets you share data among applications and move towards *document-centric* computing. If you're like most users, you've been working in an *application-centric* manner. For example, let's say you wanted to include an Excel table or chart in a Word document. Taking an application-centric approach, you would write the report in Word, move to Excel to create the table or chart, copy the table or chart to the Clipboard, move back to Word, position the insertion point, and, finally, paste the table or chart into the document. Notice that you had to bounce back and forth among the applications (Word to Excel and back to Word.) With OLE 2.0, you can perform this same procedure without leaving the comfort of Word! Rather than working around your applications, your applications begin to work around you. In sessions 2 and 3, we will explain OLE technology in greater detail.

WORKING WITH MULTIPLE APPLICATIONS

With Windows' multitasking capabilities, you can load and work with multiple application programs concurrently. Multitasking distributes the computer's processing time among running applications, ensuring that each program gets its fair, or required, share. The Windows program responsible for playing administrator, traffic cop, and tour guide is called the **Task Manager**. This section describes how you use the Task Manager to switch among programs and better organize your desktop.

MULTITASKING

Multitasking in Windows is controlled using the Task Manager. Task Manager enables you to list running applications, move among them, arrange application windows on the desktop, and close applications. To display the Task Manager, you press (Ctrl)+(Esc) or double-click on an empty area (the background) of the desktop. You can also choose the Switch To command from most Application Control Menus (▣).

To move quickly among running applications, you can bypass the Task Manager window altogether by holding down the (Alt) key while you press (Tab). With each press of the (Tab) key, the name of a running application appears on a message board in the middle of the screen. When the desired application appears, release the (Alt) key to move to that application.

Perform the following steps on your computer:

1. Turn on the power switches to the computer and monitor. The C:\> prompt or a menu appears announcing that your computer has successfully loaded the Disk Operating System (DOS). (*Note*: Your computer may automatically load Microsoft Windows when it is first turned on. If this is the case, you can skip to Step 3.)

2. To start Microsoft Windows from the C:\> prompt:
   TYPE: win
   PRESS: (Enter)
   After a few seconds, the Windows logo appears on the screen followed by the Program Manager window (Figure 1.2). (*Note*: The icons in your Program Manager window will not be exactly the same as shown in Figure 1.2. Icons represent the programs stored on your hard disk.)

Figure 1.2

The Program
Manager window.

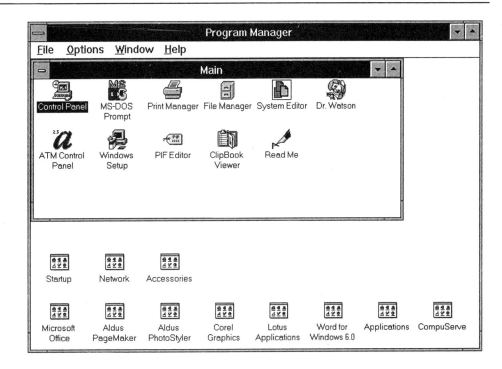

3. The Microsoft Office Manager (MOM) is typically placed into the Startup group during Office's installation process. As you're probably aware, any program item that appears in the Startup group is automatically launched each time you start Windows. Therefore, you should see MOM appear at the top of the screen, similar to the following:

The icons in your MOM's toolbar may appear slightly different that those shown above. You will learn how to customize the display of the toolbar later in this session. Or, you may see MOM appear in its own window as follows:

If MOM does not appear on your screen at all, do the following:
DOUBLE-CLICK: Microsoft Office group icon in the Program Manager window
DOUBLE-CLICK: Microsoft Office program icon (🖑)
Figure 1.3 shows the group window for Microsoft Office Professional.

Figure 1.3

Microsoft Office
Professional's
group window.

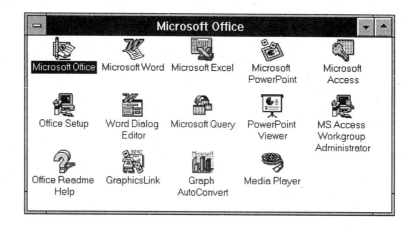

4. To load Word from the Microsoft Office Manager's toolbar:
   CLICK: Word button (🖉) once
   (*Note*: Don't double-click MOM's toolbar buttons to launch programs; a single click works just fine.)

5. Most Microsoft Office programs, such as Word 6.0, have an optional Tip of the Day dialog box that appears when they are first launched. If this dialog box appears, do the following:
   PRESS: (Enter) or CLICK: OK
   (*Note*: You can easily turn this feature off by deselecting the Show Tips at Startup check box.) You should have a blank Word document on the screen. Notice that MOM stays visible above the Microsoft Word application window.

6. Ensure that the Word application window is maximized before proceeding.

7. To practice multitasking, let's load Microsoft Excel from MOM:
   CLICK: Excel button (🖉)
   You should now have two applications (Word and Excel) open and running in memory, along with the Program Manager.

8. Ensure that the Excel application window is maximized.

9. To call up the Task Manager:
   PRESS: (Ctrl)+(Esc)
   The following window (Figure 1.4) will appear:

Figure 1.4

The Windows Task Manager.

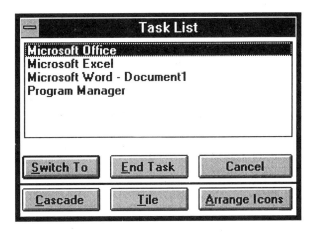

10. To move to the Program Manager:
    DOUBLE-CLICK: Program Manager in the Task List
    (*Note*: You can also highlight "Program Manager" and then select the
    Switch To command button.)

11. To move to Word's application window:
    PRESS: [Alt] and hold it down
    PRESS: [Tab] repeatedly until you see Microsoft Word appear on the
    message board (as shown below)

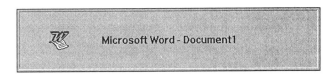

12. RELEASE: [Alt]
    The Word application window immediately comes to the foreground.

Quick Reference	•	PRESS: [Ctrl]+[Esc] to access the Task Manager
Moving Among	•	PRESS: [Alt]+[Tab] to cycle through the running applications
Multiple Applications	•	DOUBLE-CLICK: the desktop to access the Task Manager

ORGANIZING YOUR DESKTOP

You organize the running applications on your desktop in the same way that you would organize multiple group windows in the Program Manager or multiple document windows in an application. In this section, you practice minimizing, maximizing, cascading, tiling, and manipulating application windows. Although you may be familiar with these commands, the associated skills for organizing your desktop are crucial to your success in later sessions.

Perform the following steps.

1. Access the Task Manager:
    PRESS: Ctrl +Esc

2. In the Task List:
    DOUBLE-CLICK: Program Manager

3. Minimize the Program Manager window:
    CLICK: Minimize icon (▼) for the Program Manager

4. Again, let's access the Task Manager:
    PRESS: Ctrl +Esc

5. To tile the open application windows on the screen:
    SELECT: Tile command button
    Notice that the Program Manager window was not tiled with the other applications; only open windows are arranged on the desktop and we minimized the Program Manager in Step 3.

6. Now arrange the windows to appear similar to Figure 1.5. (*Hint:* To change the size or shape of a window, you drag its borders. To move a window, you drag its Title bar.) Don't worry about MOM's icons appearing over Excel's Title bar. You'll learn how to manipulate MOM in the next section.

Figure 1.5

Tiling application
windows on the
desktop.

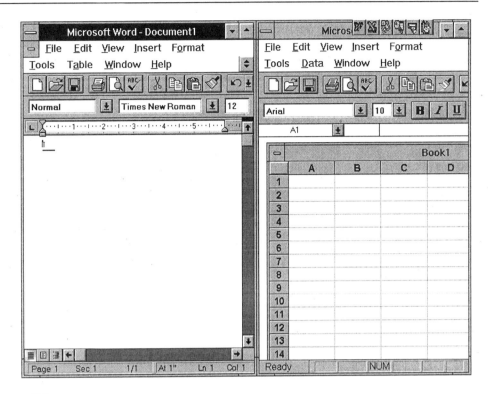

Program
Manager

7. Access the Task Manager:
    PRESS: [Ctrl]+[Esc]

8. To cascade the open application windows on the screen:
    SELECT: Cascade command button
    Your screen should now appear similar to Figure 1.6.

Figure 1.6

Cascading
application windows
on the desktop.

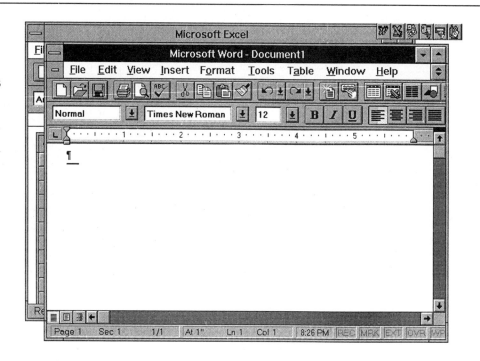

Program
Manager

9. Minimize all the open windows:
    CLICK: Minimize icon (▾) on Word's application window
    CLICK: Minimize icon (▾) on Excel's application window
    The three program icons for Program Manager, Word, and Excel
    should appear along the bottom of the screen.

10. To access the Task Manager using the mouse:
    DOUBLE-CLICK: the middle of the desktop (on an empty area)

11. SELECT: Tile command button
    Notice that nothing happens when all the programs are minimized.
    Again, only the open application windows are affected by the Tile and
    Cascade commands in the Task Manager.

12. DOUBLE-CLICK: the middle of the desktop (on an empty area)

13. You can also use the Task Manager to close an application without having to first move to the application. For example:
SELECT: Microsoft Excel in the Task List
(*Note*: Click once on "Microsoft Excel" or use the ⬆ and ⬇ arrow keys to highlight the application's name.)

14. To close Microsoft Excel:
SELECT: End Task command button
Because we did not create a worksheet, the application is immediately closed without asking for confirmation.

15. To restore Word to a window on the desktop:
DOUBLE-CLICK: Word program icon

16. Ensure that Word's application window is maximized before proceeding to the next section.

Quick Reference   1. PRESS: Ctrl + Esc to access the Task Manager
Tiling and Cascading 2. SELECT: Tile command button, or
Application Windows   SELECT: Cascade command button

GETTING TO KNOW YOUR MOM

The Microsoft Office Manager (MOM) provides access to all of the primary components of Office. In addition to acting as a launch pad for applications, MOM features a specialized Help facility that explains ways to use Office applications together. In this section, you learn how to use and customize MOM. The following section introduces the Help facility.

USING MOM

After a typical installation of Microsoft Office, MOM's program icon appears in both the Startup and Microsoft Office group windows. When first loaded, MOM appears as a row of small buttons at the top of the screen. A nice feature of MOM's toolbar is that it always appears on top of other windows, so you can't misplace it. In a maximized application window, these buttons fit nicely on the Title bar to the left of the Minimize (▾) and Restore (⬍) icons.

You use MOM's toolbar like any other toolbar. To access a feature or program, you click the desired button. For example, you can start Microsoft PowerPoint by clicking the PowerPoint button (⬛) once. (*Note*: Many people double-click the toolbar buttons unnecessarily to start applications.) If an application is already loaded when you click its button, the Office Manager assumes the role of Task Manager and switches you to the desired application. You can also launch applications from the Microsoft Office menu, accessed by clicking the Office button (⬛). Table 1.2 describes the toolbar buttons that appear by default in Microsoft Office Professional. Remember that these buttons may appear slightly different that those on your screen. You'll learn how to customize their appearance in the next session.

Table 1.2	*Button*	*Description*
MOM's Buttons	⬛	Launches Microsoft Word 6.0 for Windows.
	⬛	Launches Microsoft Excel 5.0 for Windows.
	⬛	Launches Microsoft PowerPoint 4.0 for Windows.
	⬛	Launches Microsoft Access 2.0 for Windows.
	⬛	Launches Microsoft Mail for Windows.
	⬛	Displays the Microsoft Office Manager's menu.

Perform the following steps to use MOM's toolbar.

1. Since you've already loaded Word in the last exercise, let's restart Excel using MOM's toolbar:
    CLICK: Excel button (⬛) once

2. Ensure that the Excel application window is maximized.

3. To switch back to Word without using the Task Manager:
    CLICK: Word button (⬛) once

4. To switch to Excel using the Microsoft Office menu:
    CLICK: Office button (🖻) once
    CHOOSE: Microsoft Excel from the menu

5. To switch back to Word using the keyboard method:
    PRESS: (Alt) and hold it down
    PRESS: (Tab) until you see Microsoft Word on the message board
    RELEASE: (Alt)

Another useful feature is the Find File command, found on the Office menu. You use Find File to search your disk or disks for files matching specific criteria. This command is especially important for people who save their data on a network. Not only can you tell the Find File command exactly where to look for files, you can also save your search criteria. So the next time you misplace a file on that 2 GB hard drive, remember Office's Find File command!

CUSTOMIZING MOM

MOM's toolbar is comparable to a stripped-down version of the Program Manager. To use the toolbar successfully for launching and moving among multiple applications, you need to add buttons for those programs that you use most frequently. In the following exercise, you learn how to customize the positioning and display of MOM's toolbar and how to add and remove application buttons.

Perform the following steps.

1. To display a context-sensitive menu for MOM, position the mouse pointer over any button on the toolbar and click the right mouse button once.

2. To change the size of the buttons displayed in the toolbar:
    CHOOSE: Large Buttons
    The toolbar floats away from the top of the screen in its own window, complete with a Control menu (🖃) and a Minimize icon (▾).

3. Practice moving and sizing MOM's toolbar by dragging its Title bar and borders. For example, shape the toolbar as follows:

4. Reshape the toolbar to appear as the figure shown below:

5. To customize the toolbar using the menu:
    CLICK: Office button ( )
    A menu (Figure 1.7) should appear on the screen. (*Note*: Depending on where the toolbar is situated, the menu may appear to sprout upwards rather than drop down.)

Figure 1.7

MOM's menu.

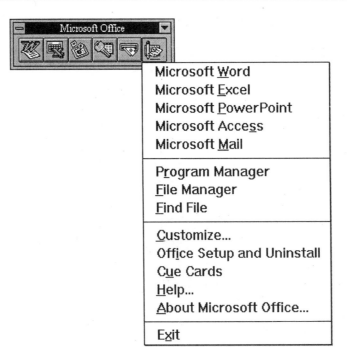

6. To customize the toolbar:
   CHOOSE: Customize from the menu
   A dialog box with three tabs—Toolbar, Menu, and View—appears, as shown in Figure 1.8. The Toolbar and Menu tabs let you add new programs to MOM in the form of toolbar buttons and menu options. Using the View tab, you can set MOM's default button size and specify whether the toolbar should always appear on top of other windows.

Figure 1.8

MOM's Customize dialog box and tabs.

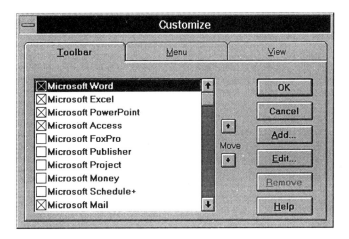

7. To add two new buttons to the toolbar, select the Toolbar tab and then scroll down the list box for the desired options. Do the following:
   SELECT: Toolbar tab
   SELECT: File Manager check box
   SELECT: Task Manager check box
   (*Note*: You can also add programs that do not appear in the list box by clicking the Add command button. In the dialog box that appears, you specify a program in much the same way that you set up a new program item in the Program Manager.)

8. To display the Task Manager button before (to the left of) the File Manager button on the toolbar, you must move the Task Manager option above File Manager in the list box. Do the following:
   SELECT: Task Manager option in the list box
   CLICK: Move Up arrow (⬛) repeatedly until Task Manager appears one line above File Manager in the list box

9. CLICK: OK command button
   Your toolbar should now appear similar to the following:

10. To prove that the new buttons actually work:
    CLICK: Task Manager button ( )
    The Task Manager window appears.

11. To close Excel using the Task Manager:
    SELECT: Microsoft Excel
    SELECT: End Task command button

12. To remove the Task Manager from MOM's toolbar:
    CLICK: Office button ( )
    CHOOSE: Customize
    SELECT: Toolbar tab

13. To turn off the display of the Task Manager button in the toolbar:
    SELECT: Task Manager option so that no × appears in its check box

14. PRESS: Enter or CLICK: OK

15. To restore the toolbar display so that it appears at the top of the screen:
    RIGHT-CLICK: MOM's toolbar
    CHOOSE: Small Buttons

Quick Reference	1.	CLICK: Office button ( )
Customizing MOM's	2.	CHOOSE: Customize from the menu
Toolbar	3.	SELECT: Toolbar tab to add buttons to the toolbar
		SELECT: Menu tab to add options to Office's drop-down menu
		SELECT: View tab to change the display size of toolbar buttons

GETTING HELP

Similar to most applications, Microsoft Office provides a comprehensive on-line Help facility. To access help, you choose the Help command from the Office menu. The resulting Help window (appearing to the right) provides four options directly related to Microsoft Office and an additional set of application-specific topics. You can browse the contents by clicking on any words and phrases that are green and have a solid underline. These are called **jump terms** because they allow you to jump quickly to topics of interest. Words or phrases that are green and have a dotted underline provide definition boxes when they are clicked. Once displayed, you remove the definition by clicking the box a second time.

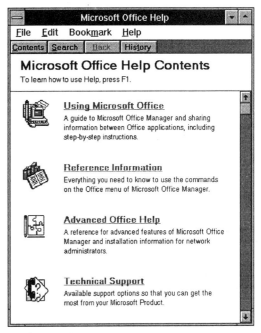

Microsoft Office also provides Cue Cards that stay visible on the screen while leading you through step-by-step instructions for common integration tasks, such as performing a mail merge between Word and Access. You access these Cue Cards by choosing the Cue Cards command from the Office menu.

Perform the following steps.

1. To display the Help facility for Microsoft Office:
   CLICK: Office button ()
   CHOOSE: Help

2. SELECT: Using Microsoft Office jump term
   In other words, position the mouse pointer over the "Using Microsoft Office" jump term until it becomes a hand (🖑) and click once.

3. Under the Using Microsoft Office Manager topic area:
    SELECT: Displaying Cue Card Instructions As You Work
    You are immediately taken to a help topic on accessing Cue Cards.
    (*Note*: If you find a helpful topic, you can either read it on-screen or
    print it using the File, Print Topic command.)

4. After reading the help topic, return to the table of contents:
    CLICK: Contents command button (below the Menu bar)

5. To exit the Help facility:
    CHOOSE: File, Exit

6. · Let's access the Office Cue Cards using the context-sensitive menu:
    RIGHT-CLICK: any button on MOM's toolbar
    CHOOSE: Cue Cards
    The Microsoft Office Cue Cards window appears, as shown in Figure
    1.9 below.

Figure 1.9

An example of a
Cue Card.

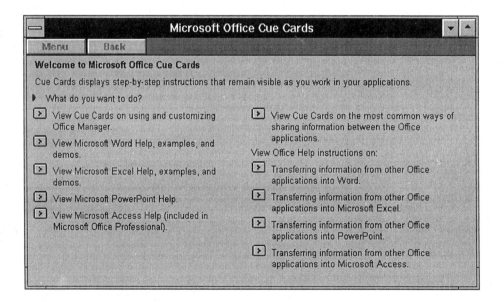

---

7. Position the mouse pointer over the greater than symbol (▶) to the left
    of the "View Cue Cards on using and customizing Office Manager."

8. When the mouse pointer becomes a hand (🖑), click the mouse button.

9. To peruse the topic on adding a button to MOM's toolbar:
   SELECT: Customize the Office Manager toolbar.
   SELECT: Add a button to the toolbar.

10. After reading the topic, close the Cue Cards:
    DOUBLE-CLICK: Cue Card's Application Control Menu (▤)
    (*Note*: You can also press [Alt]+[F4] to close a Help window or a Cue
    Card window.)

Quick Reference *Accessing Office's Help Facility*	1. CLICK: Office button (▣)
	2. CHOOSE: Help or Cue Cards to access two different types of help
	3. SELECT: Help topic jump terms to find the desired help information
	4. DOUBLE-CLICK: Help Window's Application Control Menu (▤) to exit the Help facility

SUMMARY

Microsoft Office is an application suite of the most popular applications for Windows, including Microsoft Word 6.0, Microsoft Excel 5.0, Microsoft PowerPoint 4.0, Microsoft Access 2.0 (Professional Edition only), and a Microsoft Mail workstation license. The increasing popularity of software suites is a direct result of more people using more applications on their desktop computers. Sophisticated computer users now demand consistency and integration among their applications. Because many of the skills learned in one application are transferable to the next application, novice computer users find suites faster to learn and easier to use.

This session described the individual components that comprise Microsoft Office, including the Microsoft Office Manager (MOM). In addition to reviewing the Task Manager and how to manipulate application windows on the desktop, you learned to launch applications from MOM's toolbar and customize the toolbar buttons. Lastly, this session introduced the Help facility for Microsoft Office which provides some excellent information for solving cross-application scenarios.

Table 1.3 provides a list of the commands and procedures covered in this session.

Table 1.3	*Command/Keystroke*	*Description*
Command Summary	Ctrl + Esc	Accesses the Task Manager; displays the Task List of running applications
	Alt + Tab	Cycles through the running applications on a message board allowing you to change to an application quickly
	Office (📖), Customize	Lets you customize the toolbar, Office menu, and view preferences (Small Buttons, Regular Buttons, and Large Buttons)
	Office (📖), Help	Accesses the Microsoft Office Help facility
	Office (📖), Cue Cards	Accesses the Microsoft Office Cue Cards

KEY TERMS

accelerator keys   Speed keys or shortcuts that allow you to perform a menu command by pressing a quick key combination.

ClipArt Gallery   A mini-app provided with Microsoft Office that lets you manage clip art images and insert them into other applications.

Equation Editor   A mini-app provided with Microsoft Office that lets you create and insert complex mathematical and scientific equations into other applications.

jump terms   In the Windows Help facility, a phrase that appears green with a solid underline that lets you jump from topic to topic by clicking it with the mouse.

mini-apps   Small application programs bundled with Microsoft Office and its applications. Rather than being stand-alone applications, they act as servers that provide data to the primary applications.

Object Linking and Embedding (OLE)   A technology that allows you to share data among multiple applications, regardless of the different data formats. OLE is discussed in greater detail in Sessions 2 and 3.

OfficeLinks   Procedures for sharing and integrating the applications that comprise Microsoft Office. OLE technology is a component of Microsoft OfficeLinks.

offices   A single product that bundles several individual applications together and sells them for a fraction of the total component cost. Most offices contain a word processing application, a spreadsheet, a presentation graphics program, and a database application. Also called suites.

Organization Chart   A mini-app provided with Microsoft Office that lets you create and insert organizational charts into other applications.

suites   See *offices*.

Task Manager   A Windows utility that lets you switch among running applications, organize running applications on the desktop, and close running applications.

WordArt   A mini-app provided with Microsoft Office that lets you manipulate and apply special effects to text and then insert the text into other applications.

workgroup   Two or more users connected via a network for the purpose of sharing data and working together on projects.

EXERCISES

SHORT ANSWER

1. What applications are included in the Office Professional Edition?
2. Name the mini-apps that were introduced this session.
3. Why are software suites or offices increasing in popularity?
4. How does Microsoft Office provide *consistency* among applications?
5. How does Microsoft Office provide *integration* among applications?
6. What is MOM an abbreviation for?
7. What is OLE an abbreviation for?
8. Name two methods for accessing the Task Manager.

9. Name two methods for changing the display size of buttons on the Microsoft Office Manager's toolbar.

10. What is the difference between using the Help facility and Cue Cards?

HANDS-ON

1. In the following exercise, you will practice organizing applications on the desktop.
    a. Turn on your computer and load Microsoft Windows.
    b. If it is not already loaded, load the Microsoft Office Manager.
    c. Minimize the Program Manager window.
    d. Launch Microsoft Word 6.0 for Windows using MOM's toolbar.
    e. Maximize Word's application window.
    f. Launch Microsoft Excel 5.0 for Windows using MOM's toolbar.
    g. Maximize Excel's application window.
    h. Switch to Word using the toolbar.
    i. Switch to Excel using the Task Manager.
    j. Switch to the Program Manager using `Alt`+`Tab`.
    k. Using the Task Manager, cascade all the application windows including the Program Manager window.
    l. Minimize the Program Manager window.
    m. Using the Task Manager, tile the remaining application windows.
    n. Using the mouse, position the application windows to match the screen in Figure 1.10.
    o. Using the Task Manager, close Excel's application window.
    p. Close Word by double-clicking its Application Control menu (⊟).

Figure 1.10

Arranging
application windows
on the desktop.

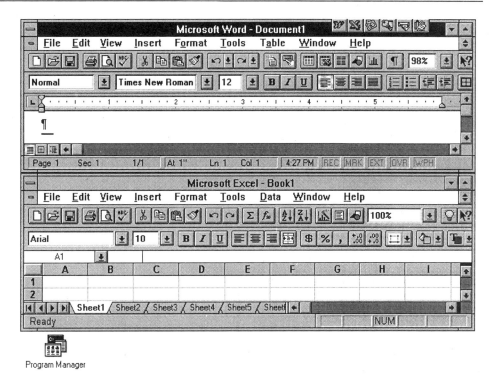

2. This exercise lets you practice customizing the Microsoft Office
    Manager's toolbar.
    a. Using the context-sensitive menu, display MOM's toolbar using
        the regular-sized buttons. (*Hint*: Right-click the toolbar.)
    b. Move the toolbar window into the middle of the screen by
        dragging its Title bar.
    c. Minimize the toolbar window.
    d. Restore the toolbar window by double-clicking its icon at the
        bottom of the screen.
    e. Display MOM's toolbar using the large-sized buttons.
    f. Add a button to the toolbar for accessing the Control Panel.
    g. Launch the Control Panel using the toolbar button.
    h. Close the Control Panel window.
    i. Remove the Control Panel button from the toolbar.
    j. If it exists, remove the File Manager button from the toolbar.
    k. Display MOM's toolbar using the small-sized buttons.
    l. Exit the Microsoft Office Manager using the Office menu (🗒).

INTEGRATING MICROSOFT OFFICE VERSION 4.2/4.3: SHARING INFORMATION

Since we were old enough to understand, most of us have been told that sharing is a "good thing." (Don't you wish your parents and teachers had been around to guide the early software developers?) Microsoft now adds a new dimension to sharing; making it, in fact, a "great thing." With Office, you can share databases with tables, tables with reports, reports with presentations, and the list goes on. In this section, you learn how to perform some common integration tasks using Word, Excel, PowerPoint, and Access.

PREVIEW

When you have completed this session, you will be able to:

Describe the different methods for sharing information.

•

Explain the difference between linking and embedding.

•

Insert an Excel chart into a Word document using drag and drop between applications.

•

Insert a linked Excel object into a Word document.

•

Create a PowerPoint presentation from a Word outline.

•

Merge a Word document with a list of names stored in an Excel table and an Access database.

SESSION OUTLINE

Why This Session Is Important
Copying and Moving Information
      Using the Clipboard
      Using Drag and Drop
      What is OLE, Anyway?
      Linking
      Embedding
      Linking Versus Embedding
Inserting and Editing Objects
      Embedding an Object
      Visual Editing
      Linking an Object
Applications Working Together
      Sharing Data Between Word and Excel
      Sharing Data Between Word and
          PowerPoint
Performing Mail Merges
      Merging with an Excel Data Source
      Merging with an Access Data Source
Summary
      Command Summary
Key Terms
Exercises
      Short Answer
      Hands-On

WHY THIS SESSION IS IMPORTANT

There has been a definite trend lately toward making software smarter. To this end, software companies have hired new staff members: Borland has Coaches, Lotus has Smart Assistants, and Microsoft has Wizards. Kidding aside, these software features make short order of the tasks you've grown accustomed to loathing. For example, mail merging a document in Microsoft Word with a database in Microsoft Access is handled almost entirely by a Wizard. You simply follow the on-screen directions to perform one of the most complicated computing procedures ever devised. Although there aren't many Microsoft Wizards employed in the field of integrating applications (other than the Mail Merge Wizard), Office has the next best thing: **OfficeLinks**.

Microsoft OfficeLinks is a set of tools and features that simplify copying and moving information amongst the Office applications. Some of these features are based on OLE technology and some are based on additional tools, but all strive to help you automate cross-application tasks. In this session, you will concentrate on working with and integrating the primary applications in Microsoft Office.

Before proceeding, make sure the following are true:

1. You have loaded the Microsoft Office Manager (MOM).
2. Your Advantage Diskette is inserted into drive A:.

COPYING AND MOVING INFORMATION

Windows enables you to easily exchange information among different applications. The three primary methods for sharing information are **pasting**, **linking**, and **embedding**. Regardless of the method, the process is very similar to a regular cut or copy and paste procedure. For instance, to copy a cell's contents from a worksheet into a word processing document, select the cell and then issue the Edit, Copy command to place it on the Clipboard. After moving to the word processing application using Alt+Tab or MOM, issue the Edit, Paste command to place a copy of the Clipboard data into the document.

USING THE CLIPBOARD

When you cut or copy information from a document, Windows places the information in a temporary storage area called the Clipboard. You can paste the contents of the Clipboard to another location in the same application or to another application. When you paste information, you are not supplying a link between applications or document files; you are simply placing a snapshot of information into the destination document. To update the pasted data in the destination document, you must repeat the process of copying from the source document. Pasting is used when you need to perform a one-time exchange of information.

The general process for copying and moving information using the Clipboard is summarized in the following steps:

a.   Select the text, graphic, or object that you want to copy or move.
b.   Cut or copy the selection to the Clipboard.
c.   Move the insertion point to where you want to place the information.
d.   Paste the information from the Clipboard into the document.
e.   Repeat steps c. and d., as desired.

Information resides on the Clipboard until it is cleared or until another piece of information is cut or copied. You can use the Clipboard Viewer program from the Main group window to view the contents of the Clipboard at any time. The Clipboard tools, common across all Microsoft Office applications, for cutting, copying, and pasting appear in Table 2.1.

Table 2.1	*Menu Command*	*Toolbar Button*	*Keyboard Shortcut*	*Description*
Copying and Moving Information Using the Clipboard	Edit, Cut	✂	Ctrl+x	Moves the selected object from the document to the Clipboard.
	Edit, Copy	📋	Ctrl+c	Copies the selected object to the Clipboard.
	Edit, Paste	📋	Ctrl+v	Inserts the contents of the Clipboard at the insertion point.

Quick Reference	• To move information using the Clipboard: CHOOSE: Edit, Cut or click the Cut button (✂)
Copying and	
Moving Information	• To copy information using the Clipboard: CHOOSE: Edit, Copy or click the Copy button (📋)
Using the Clipboard	
	• To paste information using the Clipboard: CHOOSE: Edit, Paste or click the Paste button (📋)

USING DRAG AND DROP

The drag and drop method is the easiest and most intuitive way to copy and move information short distances. The Clipboard is not used during a drag and drop operation; therefore, you can only copy or move a selection from one location to another. In other words, you are not able to perform multiple "pastes" of the selection. This method works well for simple "from-here-to-there" copy and move operations.

In addition to using drag and drop within an application, OLE 2.0 technology now lets you use drag and drop to copy and move objects between applications. To perform drag and drop copying, select an object (for example, an Excel chart), drag it to its destination in another application window (perhaps, a Word document), and then release the mouse button to drop it into place.

WHAT IS OLE, ANYWAY?

OLE is an acronym for Object Linking and Embedding, a technology that facilitates sharing and transferring data among Windows-based applications. OLE enables you to move from application-centric computing, where you perform a specific task in a specific application, to document-centric computing, where you perform a specific task using whatever applications are necessary. Before proceeding, you should be familiar with the following terms:

- The document in which the data was first composed, before being transferred to a compound document, is called a **source document**.
- The application that you use to create the source document is called the **server application**.
- A document that receives data from another application is called a **compound document** or a destination document.
- The application that accepts data into its compound document is called the **client application**.

In the following diagram (Figure 2.1), the two server applications (Microsoft Excel and Microsoft Word) are providing the data from their source documents to the compound document in the client application (Microsoft PowerPoint.) For more detailed definitions on linking and embedding terminology, refer to Table 2.2.

Figure 2.1

Diagram showing source documents serving a compound document.

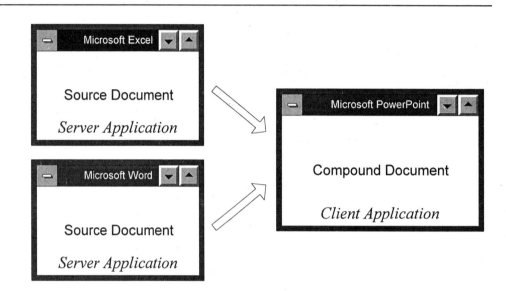

Table 2.2	*Term*	*Definition*
Definitions: Object Linking and Embedding Technology	Object	Any type of data, such as a document, table, chart, database, slide, sound file, or video clip, that has been linked or embedded into a document. An OLE object can be an entire file or a part of a file.
	Linking	The process of inserting an object into a compound document. With linking, only the location of the object's source document is actually stored in the compound document.
	Embedding	The process of inserting an object into a compound document. With embedding, the object's data is stored in the compound document along with the name of the server application.

	Term	Definition
Table 2.2 Continued		
	Server Application	The application that provides objects for linking or embedding into compound documents. For example, Excel is the server application for worksheet tables and charts presented and stored in a Microsoft Word compound document. (*Note:* An application can be both a client and a server.)
	Client Application	The application used to create a compound document. A client application accepts linked or embedded objects from server applications. For example, Microsoft Word is commonly a client for Excel tables and charts. (*Note:* An application can be both a client and a server.)
	Compound Document	A single document that contains data in several different formats; for example, a Word document may contain a bitmap graphic, an Excel table, a sound file, and a video clip.

LINKING

Rather than using the Clipboard's static method for pasting information, you can use the Edit, Paste Special command to establish a link between a source and a compound document. When you make changes in the source document (using the server application), the information in the linked compound document (in the client application) is automatically updated.

You link files when the information you need from a source document is also used by other compound documents. For example, you may have a monthly sales forecast that you need included in several related reports. In this case, linking the compound report documents to the one source document is the most efficient method for automatically updating the reports when the forecast changes. As you may expect, linking is also very useful for sharing information with workgroups over a network.

EMBEDDING

Embedding information involves inserting an object into a compound document (client application) from a source document (server application). Unlike a linked object, an embedded object does not retain a connection to the source document; everything is contained in the compound document. Therefore, an embedded object is not automatically updated when information in its source document changes.

LINKING VERSUS EMBEDDING

To the person reading or using a compound document, linked and embedded objects appear identical. The primary difference between a linked object and an embedded object is where the data is stored. With a linked object, the data remains in the original source document file and the client application stores only a reference to the file in the compound document. With an embedded object, the data is stored in the compound document file along with information about the server application.

To determine which method you should use for inserting objects, review the comments in Table 2.3 and then ask yourself these questions:

- "How am I going to use the information?"
- "Who else needs the information?"
- "Who is responsible for updating the information?"

Table 2.3	*Link an Object When...*	*Embed an Object When...*
Linking Versus Embedding	The information is shared among multiple users on your network.	You are the only user of the information.
	The information must be updated dynamically.	You want to edit or format the data from within the compound document.
	Disk storage space is a concern; a compound document that uses linked objects is typically much smaller than one that uses an embedded objects.	You plan on showing your presentation or giving your document to users not on your network. In other words, the source documents to which your compound document is linked are not available to them.

INSERTING AND EDITING OBJECTS

This section explains the "how to" of inserting objects. In the next section, you'll learn these same methods using a hands-on approach.

EMBEDDING AN OBJECT

To insert a new object, position the insertion point in the document and choose the Insert, Object command. From the dialog box that appears (Figure 2.2), select an object type on the Create New tab and click OK to proceed. The selected object's server application is launched and you may begin creating the object that you want to insert into the current document.

Figure 2.2

One example of the Object dialog box.

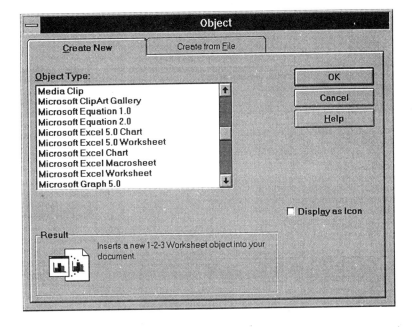

There are two methods for returning to the document after you've finished creating the object. If the server application supports visual editing, you simply click in the document outside of the object's frame. If, however, the server application launched itself in a separate window, choose the File, Exit and Return to Document command. When asked to update the object in the document, select Yes command button or press (Enter).

To insert an existing object, you can use one of the following methods:

- Choose the Edit, Copy command to place the object on the Clipboard and then choose Edit, Paste after positioning the insertion point in the destination document. If both applications are OLE-aware (that is, they support OLE features), the information is automatically embedded.

- Choose the Edit, Copy command to place the object on the Clipboard and then choose Edit, Paste Special. From the dialog box, select the first option in the As list box (usually the object type.)

- Choose the Insert, Object command and select the Create from File tab to specify the desired file name.

- Drag the object from the server application's window to the compound document in the client application's window.

VISUAL EDITING

Visual Editing, a feature of OLE, makes it easy to update an embedded object in a compound document. To edit an embedded object, such as an Excel table, you simply double-click the object. Rather than being launched into the server application in order to perform the changes, you remain where you are and the current application's menus and toolbars are replaced with those of the server application. You can perform the same functions as in the original server application, and you don't have to leave the current document window!

LINKING AN OBJECT

The two methods for establishing a link between a source document and a compound document are as follows:

- Once an object is placed on the Clipboard, choose the Edit, Paste Special command to specify how it should be inserted into the document. To link the information, you select the Paste Link option in the dialog box that appears.

- Similarly to embedding an object, choose the Insert, Object command and then select the Create from File tab to specify a source document for linking. To establish the link, you select the Link to File check box before pressing (Enter) or clicking on OK.

APPLICATIONS WORKING TOGETHER

Here's what you've been waiting for! In this section, you will learn how to integrate Microsoft Office's primary applications.

SHARING DATA BETWEEN WORD AND EXCEL

Microsoft Word and Microsoft Excel work very well together. Word even places an "Insert Microsoft Excel Worksheet" button on its Standard toolbar, making it easy to insert a table of figures without leaving the comfort of Word. It is also surprisingly simple to drag and drop an object, such as a chart, between the two applications. In most scenarios, Word plays the part of the client application while Excel acts as its server.

Let's start with an exciting example of drag and drop! To demonstrate the ease with which Word and Excel exchange data, perform the following steps.

1. Load Microsoft Word 6.0 and Microsoft Excel 5.0. Ensure that each has a blank document or worksheet displayed.

2. Using the Task Manager, arrange the windows to appear similar to Figure 2.3.

Figure 2.3

Tiling application
windows on the
desktop.

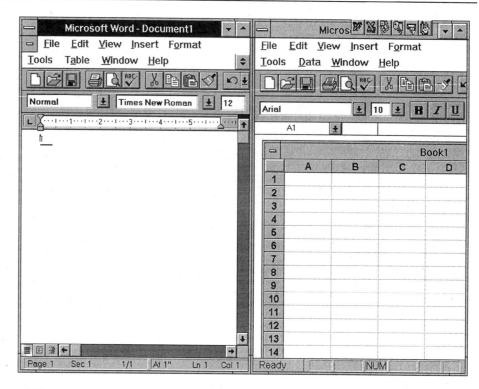

Program
Manager

3. In Excel, load the CRUISES worksheet. This worksheet includes a small table of values and a chart.

4. To copy the chart between applications using drag and drop, position the mouse pointer over the chart and do the following:
    PRESS: Ctrl and hold it down
    CLICK: the chart and hold down the left mouse button
    DRAG: the chart from the Excel worksheet to the Word document
    Notice that the mouse pointer changes as you move it over top of the Word document.

5. Position the mouse pointer at the top of the document and release the mouse button. The chart is immediately embedded into the Word document. (*Note*: You would perform the same steps to move a chart, except you do not hold down the Ctrl key.) Your screen should now appear similar to Figure 2.4.

Figure 2.4

Drag and drop
copying between
applications.

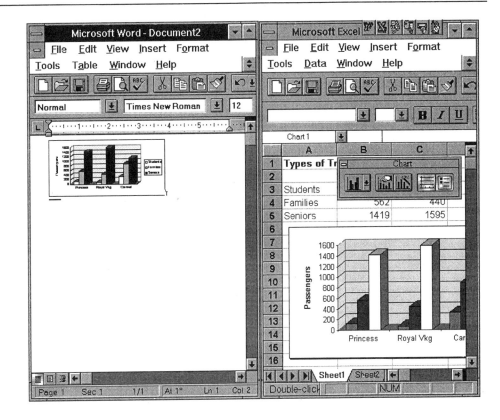

Now you will practice linking an Excel table with a Word document. Perform the following steps.

1. Make Excel the active application. (*Hint*: Click once on its Title bar.)

2. SELECT: the cell range from A1 to D5

3. To copy this information to the Clipboard:
    CHOOSE: Edit, Copy from the Excel menu

4. Make Word the active application.

5. Position the insertion point to the left of the chart object (do not select the chart) and then do the following:
    PRESS: ⟨Enter⟩ three times to insert three blank lines at the top of the document

6. In the next few steps, you paste the contents of the Clipboard into the document and establish a live link to the Excel file. Move to the top of the document.

7. To set up the link between the Word object and the Excel worksheet:
CHOOSE: Edit, Paste Special from the Word menu
SELECT: Paste Link option button
SELECT: Formatted Text (RTF) in the As list box
The Paste Special dialog box appears, as shown in Figure 2.5.

Figure 2.5

Paste Special
dialog box.

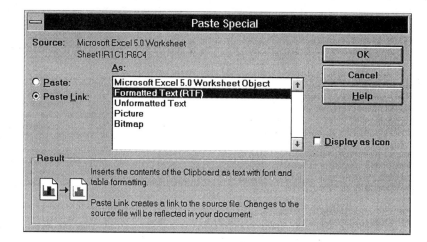

8. To complete the operation:
PRESS: [Enter] or CLICK: OK

9. Let's prove that the Word object is linked to the Excel worksheet. To begin, make Excel the active application.

10. Enter a new value for the Student travelers on Princess lines:
SELECT: cell B3
TYPE: 1150
PRESS: [Enter]
You may have noticed two things when you modified the value in cell B3. First, the Word table object was immediately updated since it is linked. Second, the graph in Excel changed to reflect the new value, but the embedded chart did not change since it is not linked. Your screen should now look similar to Figure 2.6.

Figure 2.6

Linking and embedding objects between Word and Excel.

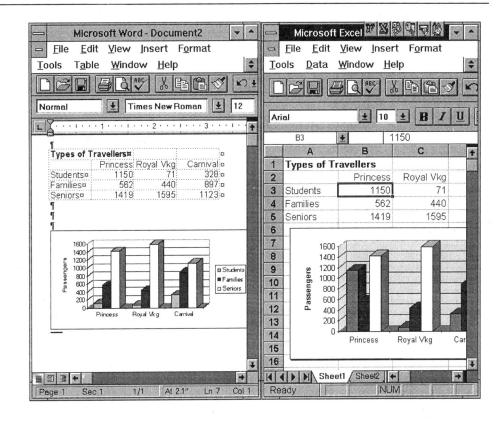

11. Practice changing some other numbers in the worksheet before continuing.

12. Remove the chart from the Word document by selecting it and then pressing the (**Delete**) key.

13. Copy the new chart from the Excel worksheet to the Word document using drag and drop.

14. Close the documents and do not save them.

15. Close Excel before proceeding to the next section.

Quick Reference	1.	Copy or cut the desired information to the Clipboard from the
Pasting and Linking		source document.
Information	2.	Move the insertion point to the compound or destination document.
	3.	CHOOSE: Edit, Paste Special
	4.	SELECT: Paste Link option button
	5.	PRESS: (Enter) or CLICK: OK

SHARING DATA BETWEEN WORD AND POWERPOINT

There are several opportunities for sharing data between Microsoft Word and Microsoft PowerPoint. If you've already written an outline in Word, you can transform it into a PowerPoint slide presentation in less time than it would take to send it to the printer. If you've created a spiffy set of slides in PowerPoint, you can convert the presentation to a Word outline as the basis for a report. And these activities are additional to the normal copy and paste, drag and drop, and linking and embedding topics that we've been discussing up to this point.

Perform the following steps to automatically convert a Word outline into a PowerPoint slide presentation.

1. If it is not already loaded, launch Microsoft Word 6.0.

2. In Word, open the HARDWARE document located on the Advantage Diskette. This document provides an outline for a discussion about computer hardware.

3. There are two methods for converting a Word outline into a presentation. In PowerPoint, you can open an existing Word outline document and it will automatically convert it to a presentation. In Word, you can send an outline to PowerPoint by clicking the PresentIt button (⊞) on the Microsoft toolbar. Since you are already working in Word, let's use the toolbar method. To display the Microsoft toolbar:
    RIGHT-CLICK: any button on the Standard or Formatting toolbars
    SELECT: Microsoft from the shortcut menu
    A new toolbar appears in the application window.

4. To convert the existing outline into a slide presentation:
    CLICK: PresentIt button (⊞) on the Microsoft toolbar
    After a few moments, PowerPoint's outline view appears, as shown in Figure 2.7. Notice that the six main topics (formatted using the Heading 1 style in Word) have become the titles for six slides in a new PowerPoint presentation. All text formatted using the Heading 2 style in Word has been transformed into bullet points on the six slides.

Figure 2.7

Converting a Word outline into a PowerPoint presentation.

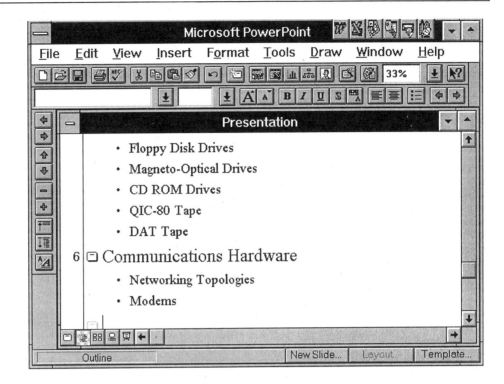

5. To make the presentation more attractive:
   CLICK: Template button on the Status bar
   SELECT: clrovrhd from the Directories list box
   SELECT: bludiagc.ppt from the File Name list box
   PRESS: [Enter] or CLICK: Apply

6. To display the slides as they will be seen by your audience:
   SELECT: Slide View button (⬜) at the left-hand side of the horizontal scroll bar

7. Save the presentation as HARDWARE.PPT to the Advantage Diskette.

Quick Reference	1. Open the Word document containing the desired outline.
Creating a	2. Display the Microsoft toolbar in the Word application window.
PowerPoint Slide	3. CLICK: PresentIt button (▣) on the Microsoft toolbar
Presentation From	4. Format the presentation in PowerPoint.
a Word Outline	

PowerPoint allows you to copy entire slides, or individual objects from a slide, into a Word document or an Excel worksheet. This feature may become important to you if you've added special objects, such as tables, charts, and graphics, to your slides and need to use them elsewhere. To practice copying an entire slide from a PowerPoint presentation into a Word document, perform the following steps.

1. Using the vertical scroll bar, move to the slide titled "Output Hardware" in the HARDWARE presentation.

2. To copy the slide to the Clipboard:
   CHOOSE: Edit, Select All
   CHOOSE: Edit, Copy
   (*Note*: The Edit, Select All command selects all of the objects on the slide. However, there is no way to select the background template.)

3. Move to the HARDWARE document in Word.

4. To display the document in Normal view:
   CLICK: Normal View button (■) on the horizontal scroll bar

5. In Word, position the insertion point immediately below the heading "Output Hardware."

6. Add two blank lines and then move the insertion point below the heading "Output Hardware" once again.

7. To paste the slide into the Word document:
   CHOOSE: Edit, Paste
   Notice that the slide covers the entire width of the page. You will also notice that the entire contents of the slide were copied, except for the background template.

8. To size the slide:
   CLICK: *anywhere on the slide*
   DRAG: the sizing corner until the slide covers half of the page

9. Close the document without saving the changes.

10. Close PowerPoint 4.0 without saving the changes to the HARDWARE presentation.

Quick Reference	1.	Open the PowerPoint presentation and move to the desired slide.
Displaying a	2.	CHOOSE: Edit, Select All from the PowerPoint menu
PowerPoint Slide in	3.	CHOOSE: Edit, Copy from the PowerPoint menu
a Word Document	4.	Position the insertion point in the Word document.
	5.	CHOOSE: Edit, Paste to insert the slide into the document

PERFORMING MAIL MERGES

One of the most powerful features of word processing software is the ability to merge names and addresses into standard documents for printing. This process, called **mail merge**, allows you to create a single document and then print personalized copies for numerous recipients. Mail merge activities are not limited, however, to producing form letters. Merging can be used to print a batch of invoices, promotional letters, or legal contracts.

Merging requires two files: the **data source** and the **main document**. The data source contains the variable data, such as names and addresses, to be merged with the main document or form letter. In this section, you perform two separate mail merges. In the first scenario, you merge an existing Word document with a list of names stored as a database in an Excel worksheet. In the second scenario, you merge the same Word document with selected records from an Access database. You will use Microsoft Word, Microsoft Excel, Microsoft Access, and Microsoft Query in this section. Microsoft Query is a program designed to filter and withdraw information from both Excel and Access databases.

MERGING WITH AN EXCEL DATA SOURCE

To merge a Word form letter with information stored in an Excel worksheet, perform the following steps.

1. Load Microsoft Word 6.0 and Microsoft Excel 5.0 using MOM. Ensure that each has a blank document or worksheet displayed. (Make sure that you've closed PowerPoint before proceeding.)

2. In Word, open the PROMO document located on the Advantage Diskette. This document is a standard form letter that you'll modify to merge with an Excel data source.

3. To begin the mail merge:
    CHOOSE: Tools, Mail Merge from the Word menu
    You should see the Mail Merge Helper dialog box appear.

4. The Mail Merge Helper provides three steps as a checklist for performing a mail merge. The first step, according to the dialog box, is to create or specify a main document file. To proceed:
    SELECT: Create button under the Main Document area
    CHOOSE: Form Letters from the pop-up menu
    SELECT: Active Window command button
    Your Mail Merge Helper should appear similar to Figure 2.8.

Figure 2.8

Mail Merge Helper
dialog box after
selecting the Main
Document.

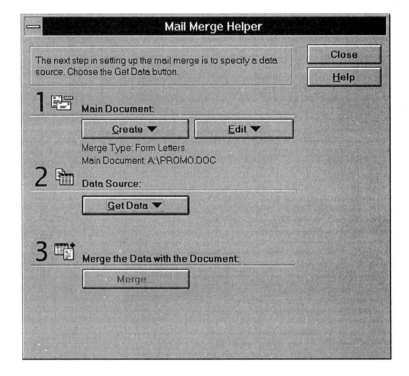

5. To complete the second step:
    SELECT: Get Data button under the Data Source area
    CHOOSE: Open Data Source

6. In the dialog box that appears:
    SELECT: MS Excel Worksheets (*.xls) in the List Files of Type drop-down list
    SELECT: a: from the Drives drop-down list
    SELECT: clients.xls in the File Name list box
    PRESS: (Enter) or CLICK: OK

7. After a few moments, a new dialog box appears asking you to specify the range of worksheet cells that contain the database. Since the entire spreadsheet file is a database and the option is already highlighted:
PRESS: [Enter] or CLICK: OK

8. The next dialog box to appear informs you that there are no merge fields in the main document:
SELECT: Edit Main Document button

9. Using the Insert Merge Field button appearing at the left-hand side of the Merge toolbar, create a merge document that matches Figure 2.9.

Figure 2.9

The Main Document with merge fields.

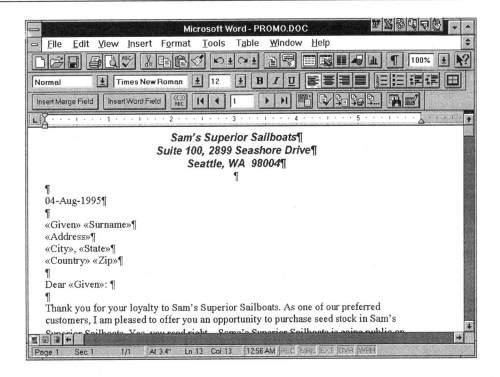

10. Once the data source file and the main document have been created or specified, you are ready to perform the merge. The output of the merge is typically sent to a new document or to the printer. If there are only a few records in the data source file, you may prefer to merge to a new document, save the document for review, and then print the document at a later time. If there are several hundred records in the data source file, merging directly to the printer is probably your best option. To merge the names from the Excel worksheet into the form letter:
CLICK: Merge to New Document button (■) in the Merge toolbar

11. After a few seconds the new document appears with the first record merged onto page 1 of the form letter. Scrolling down the document will reveal the remaining merged letters. Save this new document as FORMLTR to the Advantage Diskette.

12. Close the FORMLTR document and the PROMO document, without saving the changes.

Quick Reference	1. CHOOSE: Tools, Mail Merge
Performing a Mail	2. Specify a main document file.
Merge Using an	3. Specify an Excel worksheet file as the data source.
Excel Data Source	4. Specify the desired worksheet range (or the entire spreadsheet file) containing the data for merging.
	5. Edit the main document, inserting merge fields as desired.
	6. On the Merge toolbar, select either the Merge to New Document button or the Merge to Printer button.

MERGING WITH AN ACCESS DATA SOURCE

When you require more database power than Excel can provide, you can always turn to Access. Rather than merging all of the records stored in an Access database, you can specify particular records using Microsoft Query and a search criteria. In this section, you merge information from an Access table into a Word form letter. Perform the following steps.

1. To save memory, ensure that Microsoft Excel is closed.

2. In Word, open the PROMO document located on the Advantage Diskette. (*Note*: This is the original PROMO document, without merge fields.)

3. You begin the mail merge similar to before:
   CHOOSE: Tools, Mail Merge
   The Mail Merge Helper dialog box appears again.

4. To specify the Word merge document:
   SELECT: Create button under the Main Document area
   CHOOSE: Form Letters from the pop-up menu
   SELECT: Active Window command button

5. To specify the Data Source:
   SELECT: Get Data button under the Data Source area
   CHOOSE: Open Data Source

6. In the File Open dialog box that appears:
   SELECT: MS Query command button
   The Select Data Source dialog box appears for you to specify the type
   of data file you want Microsoft Query to access.

7. To add a new item to the Select Data Source dialog box:
   SELECT: Other command button

8. In the ODBC Data Sources dialog box (Figure 2.10):
   SELECT: MS Access 2.0 Databases
   PRESS: [Enter] or CLICK: OK

Figure 2.10

Selecting a Data
Source.

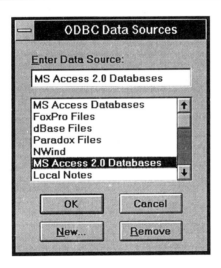

9. When asked to "Select the default database" in the next dialog box, do
   the following:
   SELECT: a: from the Drives drop-down list box
   SELECT: wedding.mdb in the File Name list box
   PRESS: [Enter] or CLICK: OK

10. When the Select Data Source dialog box reappears:
    SELECT: MS Access 2.0 Databases - Admin
    PRESS: [Enter] or CLICK: Use

11. After a few moments, the Add Tables dialog box appears. To add the Guest List table to the query:
     SELECT: Add command button
     SELECT: Close command button

12. To display the Criteria pane:
     CHOOSE: View, Criteria
     CHOOSE: Window, Tile
     Your screen should look similar to Figure 2.11.

Figure 2.11

The Query window.

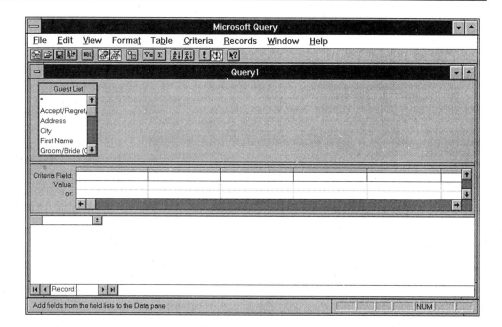

13. Position the insertion point in the Criteria Field field by clicking in it once with the mouse. You should notice that a drop-down list box arrow appears at the right-hand side of the field.

14. To specify a search criterion based on the City value in each record:
     CLICK: Criteria Field drop-down list box
     SELECT: City

15. Position the insertion point in the Values field, immediately below the Criteria field, and then do the following:
     TYPE: Walnut Grove
     You've now narrowed the search criteria to only those records where the city is Walnut Grove.

16. To finish the query, you need to select the fields that you want to draw from the Access database for use in the mail merge document. Position the insertion point in the first field or column, immediately below the Criteria pane.

17. CLICK: Field drop-down list box for Column 1
SELECT: First Name
CLICK: Field drop-down list box for Column 2
SELECT: Last Name

18. Continue selecting fields for the Address, City, State, and Zip. Each of these fields should appear in their respective columns. Notice that the values in the City column all contain "Walnut Grove," as specified in the Criteria pane.

19. To save the query:
CHOOSE: File, Save Query
TYPE: a:wedding
PRESS: [Enter] or CLICK: OK
Your screen should now look similar to Figure 2.12.

Figure 2.12

Using MS Query.

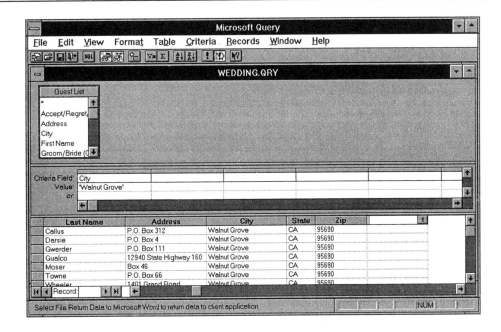

20. To return to the Word document and complete the merge:
CHOOSE: File, Return Data to Microsoft Word
You are immediately returned to the Mail Merge Helper.

21. To edit the Main Document and add merge fields:
    SELECT: Close command button

22. Using Figure 2.9 as a guide, insert the merge codes using the Insert Merge Field button on the toolbar. Notice that there is no Country field in this example.

23. To merge the names from the Access database into the form letter:
    CLICK: Merge to New Document button in the Merge toolbar

24. After a few seconds the new document appears with the first record merged onto page 1 of the form letter. Save this new document as FORMLTR1 to the Advantage Diskette.

25. Close the FORMLTR1 document and the PROMO document, without saving the changes.

26. Close all the applications and exit MOM.

Quick Reference	
Quick Reference *Using Microsoft Query to Merge a Word Document With an Access Database*	1. CHOOSE: Tools, Mail Merge 2. Specify a main document file. 3. SELECT: Get Data button under the Data Source area 4. SELECT: MS Query command button 5. Specify a data source from the Select Data Source dialog box. 6. Specify an Access table from the Add Table dialog box. 7. Specify a search criteria in the Criteria pane. 8. Specify the fields to draw from the database table. 9. Save the query and return to the Word document to complete the merge.

SUMMARY

This session discussed the various methods for sharing information in the Windows environment. Topics included using the Clipboard, drag and drop, linking, and embedding. The latter half of the session provided an opportunity to illustrate the OLE concepts in hands-on exercises. You learned how to embed an Excel object into a Word document using drag and drop, link a table of values to an Excel worksheet, create a PowerPoint presentation from a Word outline, and merge information from an Excel database and an Access database into a Word document.

Table 2.4 provides a list of the commands and procedures covered in this session.

Table 2.4	*Command*	*Description*
Command Summary	Edit, Cut (icon)	Moves the selected object from the document to the Clipboard.
	Edit, Copy (icon)	Copies the selected object to the Clipboard.
	Edit, Paste (icon)	Inserts the contents of the Clipboard at the insertion point.
	Edit, Paste Special	Inserts the contents of the Clipboard at the insertion point, but also lets you specify whether to create a link with the original source document or whether to embed the object.
	Insert, Object	Lets you create an object or insert an existing object into your document.

KEY TERMS

client application   An application that accepts data into a compound document.

compound document   A document that contains data from another application.

data source   A Word document file, Excel spreadsheet, or Access database that captures and stores variable information, such as a list of names and addresses, for the merge process.

embedding   A way of sharing and exchanging information; refers to the process of inserting an object into a compound document that is linked to the server application.

linking   A way of sharing and exchanging information; refers to the process of copying information from a source document into a compound document and establishing a dynamic link between the two.

mail merge   A procedure that typically involves combining data that is stored in a data file with a form letter created in a word processing software program.

main document   A type of form letter document used by Word in the merge process. The main document file contains codes to insert information from the data source file.

OfficeLinks   A set of tools and features that promotes cross-application integration and sharing of data.

pasting   A way of sharing and exchanging information; refers to the process of copying static information from a source document into a destination document without linking the two documents.

server application   An application that you use to create a source document.

source document   The original document in which information is created for transfer to a compound document.

EXERCISES

SHORT ANSWER

1. What is the most common method of copying and moving information?
2. What are the accelerator keys for copying, cutting, and pasting information using the Clipboard?
3. What is an object?
4. What is a compound document?
5. How do you copy an object using drag and drop between applications?
6. How do you link an object that you've copied to the Clipboard?
7. What is meant by the term *Visual Editing*?
8. Name two methods for automatically creating a PowerPoint presentation from a Word outline.
9. Name three data source alternatives for performing a mail merge.
10. What is Microsoft Query and when would you access this program?

HANDS-ON

(*Note*: In the following exercises, save your documents onto and retrieve files from the Advantage Diskette.)

1. In this session, you created a PowerPoint presentation from a Word outline. Using the same concepts and the ReportIt button (⬚) in PowerPoint, create a Word outline from the EMPLOYEE presentation stored on the Advantage Diskette.

2. Using the mailing list information from the Students table in the Access database called TRAINING, create a new document that personalizes a copy of the COMPUTER document to each student. Save this new document as COMPMAIL to the Advantage Diskette.

INTEGRATING MICROSOFT OFFICE VERSION 4.2/4.3: WORKING WITH OBJECTS

If you performed a complete install of Office on your computer, several Microsoft mini-applications were copied to your hard disk in addition to the primary applications. These applications stay relatively unknown to novice users until they are accidentally stumbled upon. However, they are not complex, nor are they difficult to learn. In this section, you use these mini-apps to practice embedding and editing objects.

PREVIEW

When you have completed this session, you will be able to:

Use the ClipArt Gallery to organize and insert clip art images into your documents.

•

Insert a scanned photograph into a document.

•

Use Equation Editor to insert mathematical expressions.

•

Use Graph to insert charts.

•

Use Organization Chart to create and modify organizational charts and other hierarchical diagrams.

•

Use WordArt to create special effects for text.

Why This Session Is Important
Using Microsoft ClipArt Gallery 1.0
Inserting Pictures
Using Microsoft Equation Editor 1.0
Using Microsoft Graph 5.0
Using Microsoft Organization Chart 1.0
Using Microsoft WordArt 2.0
Summary
       Command Summary
Key Terms
Exercises
       Short Answer
       Hands-On

WHY THIS SESSION IS IMPORTANT

When most of us read the term "application software," we immediately visualize Word, Excel, PowerPoint, or Access. However, an important aspect of any software suite is the availability of mini-applications that add value to the primary applications. In the case of Office, Microsoft provides several **mini-apps** as servers to the primary applications, as opposed to being stand-alone, independent programs. These mini-apps enable you to create objects that may be embedded into a document, worksheet, or presentation. To find out which mini-apps are available to you, choose the Insert, Object command from any application (Word, Excel, PowerPoint, or Access) and then browse through the list of objects that appears in the dialog box (Figure 3.1.) You may also remember from Session 1 that these mini-apps are typically stored, or should we say hidden, in the MSAPPS subdirectory under \WINDOWS.

Figure 3.1

One example of the Object dialog box.

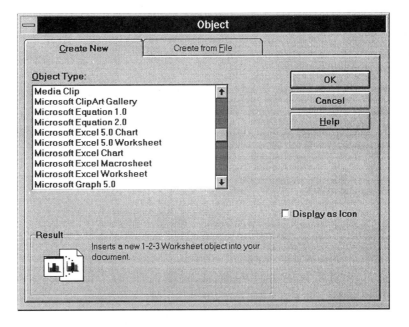

Before proceeding, make sure the following are true:

1. You have loaded the Microsoft Office Manager (MOM).
2. Your Advantage Diskette is inserted into drive A:.
3. You have loaded Microsoft Word 6.0 for Windows.

USING MICROSOFT CLIPART GALLERY 1.0

A picture is worth a thousand words! Although this phrase is overused, its truth is undeniable. Graphics add personality to your documents and convey information more efficiently than text alone. Unfortunately, many new computer users struggle with the tendency to place too many graphics on a single page. To assist your planning of how and when to use graphics, apply these basic principles: strive for simplicity, use emphasis sparingly, and ensure a visual balance between graphics and text.

The Microsoft ClipArt Gallery mini-app provides a one-stop shopping mall for all your clip art images. A **clip art image** is a computer graphic or picture that you can insert into your documents, usually without having to pay royalties or licensing fees to the artist or designer. The current versions of Office Professional and ClipArt Gallery provide close to 1,100 images organized into over 25 categories. You can also use the Gallery to add your own images, delete existing images, and move images. Here are three examples of images stored in the ClipArt Gallery:

(*Note*: In the following sections, the word "documents" is used to refer to Word documents, Excel worksheets, and PowerPoint presentations.)

Perform the following steps to insert a clip art image.

1. Open the PROMO document located on the Advantage Diskette. This letter is a promotional piece for Sam's Superior Sailboats, which is offering an opportunity to loyal customers who want to purchase seed stock. Your task is to find a clip art image for the company logo and then insert it under the heading at the top of the page.

2. Position the insertion point immediately below the address line, centered on the screen.

3. To find a logo in the ClipArt Gallery:
   CHOOSE: Insert, Object

4. In the Object dialog box:
   SELECT: Create New tab
   SELECT: Microsoft ClipArt Gallery from the Object Type list box
   PRESS: (Enter) or CLICK: OK
   If this is the first time that you've run Microsoft ClipArt Gallery, you will have to wait a few minutes while the Gallery accumulates and categorizes the available clip art images. Once it has finished, you will see the dialog box in Figure 3.2 appear.

Figure 3.2

The ClipArt Gallery dialog box.

5. Rather than trying to pick one image from hundreds, you can limit your search to a group of clip art images dealing with a specific category. To begin our search for a logo for Sam's Superior Sailboats:
   SELECT: Sports & Leisure option from the Category list box

6. Scroll through the thumbnail displays to see the various Sports & Leisure images. When you are ready to proceed:
   SELECT: Life Preserver graphic
   PRESS: (Enter) or CLICK: OK
   You are immediately returned to the document.

7. To resize a graphic object after it has been inserted:
    CLICK: on the object to select it
    DRAG: the sizing handles to match the image in Figure 3.3
    CLICK: *anywhere in the document* to deselect the object
    Your screen should now appear similar to Figure 3.3.

Figure 3.3

Sizing a clip art image.

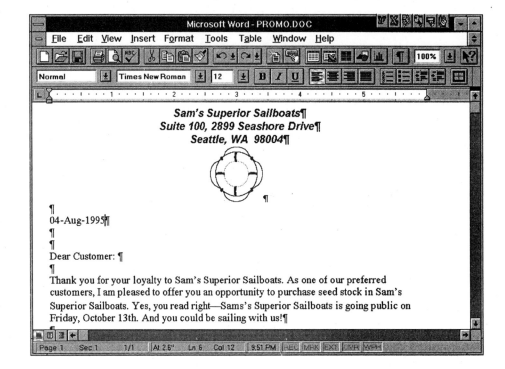

8. Save the document as SAILBOAT to the Advantage Diskette.

9. Close the document.

Quick Reference	1.	Position the insertion point where you want to insert the object.
Inserting Clip Art	2.	CHOOSE: Insert, Object
Images	3.	SELECT: Microsoft ClipArt Gallery on the Create New tab
	4.	SELECT: the Category and desired graphic
	5.	PRESS: [Enter] or CLICK: OK

INSERTING PICTURES

In addition to clip art images, you can insert graphic files into your document. A computer **graphic file** is usually created by an artist, designer, or desktop publisher. However, you can easily create your own graphic files if you have access to a **scanner**. A scanner is a hardware device that converts photographs and other paper-based material into computer images. Just as a photocopier makes a representation from paper to paper, a scanner makes a copy from paper to computer. Once saved to the disk, you can insert a computer graphic file into Word, Excel, or PowerPoint using the Insert, Picture command.

1. Open the COMPUTER document located on the Advantage Diskette. This file contains a monthly article or flyer that is designed to be given away at local computer stores. Your task is to insert a scanned photograph at the end of the document.

2. Move to the bottom of the document.

3. Make sure that there is at least one blank line between the last paragraph and the end of the document. Position the insertion point on the last line.

4. To insert a photograph that has been stored on the Advantage Diskette:
   CHOOSE: Insert, Picture
   SELECT: a: in the Drives drop-down list box
   SELECT: All Graphic Files in the List Files of Type drop-down list box
   SELECT: lab.bmp in the File Name list box
   SELECT: Preview Picture check box
   (*Caution:* Do not select the Link to File check box.) Your screen should now appear similar to Figure 3.4.

Figure 3.4

The Insert Picture
dialog box.

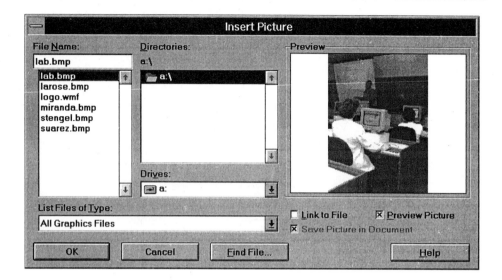

5. To proceed with inserting the graphic picture into the document:
    PRESS: (Enter) or CLICK: OK
    The graphic appears at the insertion point.

6. You size the image as you do any other object:
    CLICK: once on the image
    DRAG: the sizing handles to adjust its height and width

7. To add a caption to the graphic:
    RIGHT-CLICK: the image once
    CHOOSE: Caption from the shortcut menu

8. TYPE: : Microsoft Training at City College
    Your dialog box should appear similar to the one shown in Figure 3.5.

Figure 3.5

Preparing a caption
for the graphic.

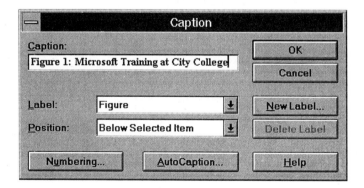

9. PRESS: [Enter] or CLICK: OK

10. Print the document. (*Note*: You can skip this step if you don't have a printer connected to your computer.)

11. Save the document as COMPUTER to the Advantage Diskette, replacing the existing version.

12. Close the document.

Quick Reference *Inserting Graphics*	1. Position the insertion point where you want to insert the object. 2. CHOOSE: Insert, Picture 3. SELECT: the desired disk drive, file type, and the file name 4. SELECT: Preview Picture check box to preview the graphic 5. PRESS: [Enter] or CLICK: OK

USING MICROSOFT EQUATION EDITOR 2.0

The Microsoft Equation Editor 2.0 mini-app allows you to insert mathematical equations into your documents without leaving your current application. Whether you are writing a paper on Quantum Physics or working in an engineering lab for Motorola, the Equation Editor provides an invaluable tool for compiling complex mathematical elements, such as fractions, exponents, and integrals, into a legible equation.

To build an equation, you select mathematical elements from over 120 templates and 150 symbols. A **template** is an empty form or framework for an equation or expression, such as a fraction. You access templates using the bottom row of buttons on the Equation Editor's toolbar (shown in Figure 3.6). A **symbol** refers to a mathematical symbol. Since these symbols are not typically found in TrueType fonts, they are provided on the top row of the Equation Editor's toolbar. When you click a button on the toolbar, a **palette** of additional options is displayed for that template or symbol.

Figure 3.6

The Equation
Editor's toolbar.

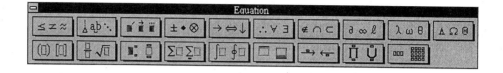

Perform the following steps to insert an equation into a document.

1. In Word, open the FINANCE document located on the Advantage Diskette. This document provides an income statement for a fictitious company. Your task in this section is to document a simple ratio that measures the company's operating results.

2. Move to the bottom of the document. In the table provided for you, position the insertion point in the second row of the first column.

3. To create a ratio that measures the net profitability of each dollar of sales, do the following:
   TYPE: Profit Margin =
   (*Note*: You are only entering the ratio into the document. Unfortunately, the Equation Editor has no ability to actually perform the calculation.)

4. PRESS: Space Bar once to insert a space between the equal sign and the new equation

5. To create the equation using the Equation Editor:
   CHOOSE: Insert, Object

6. In the Object dialog box:
   CLICK: Create New tab
   SELECT: Microsoft Equation 2.0 from the Object Type list box
   PRESS: [Enter] or CLICK: OK
   The Equation Editor toolbar and menu appear in the Word document. (*Hint*: If inserted properly, the object will be surrounded by a hatched or shaded pattern.)

7. The first step in building an equation is to select the appropriate template. Since the Profit Margin ratio is a fraction and cannot be properly created using Word's formatting styles, do the following:
   CLICK: Fraction Template button (▒▒) to display its palette and hold down the left mouse button

8. DRAG: the mouse pointer over the palette options to view their names in the Status bar
    SELECT: Full-size vertical fraction (as shown in Figure 3.7)
    When you release the mouse button, the Equation Editor inserts the selected template into your document.

Figure 3.7

Selecting the Full-size vertical fraction template from the Equation Editor's toolbar.

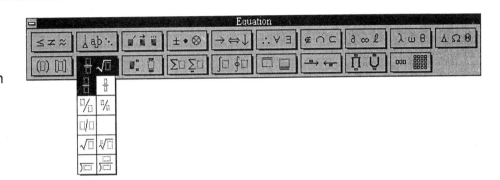

9. With the insertion point in the numerator (above the line):
    TYPE: Net Income
    PRESS: [Tab] to move to the denominator (below the line)
    TYPE: Net Sales
    Notice that the Equation Editor doesn't let you put spaces within the variables' names; they will appear as NetIncome and NetSales.

10. To insert a space manually within the word NetIncome, position the insertion point between the "t" and the "I" and then do the following:
    CLICK: Spaces & ellipses button ([⟶])
    SELECT: Thick space (one third of an em) button ([a⟋b])

11. To insert a space manually within the word NetSales, position the insertion point between the "t" and the "S" and then do the following:
    CLICK: Spaces & ellipses button ([⟶])
    SELECT: Thick space (one third of an em) button ([a⟋b])

12. To finish using the Equation Editor and return to Microsoft Word:
    CLICK: in the document, outside of the equation's frame
    (*Note*: The Visual Editing feature of OLE technology allows you to click in the document to return control to the client application, Word.)

13. Using the steps that you learned above to create the ratio, enter the values (4,750,000.00 and 1,000,000.00) in a full-size vertical fraction in the Computation and Result column. (See Figure 3.8 for a sample.)

14. Position the insertion point immediately to the right of the equation object (in the document) and do the following:
    PRESS: Space Bar
    TYPE: = .21
    Your screen should now appear similar to Figure 3.8.

Figure 3.8

The Profit Margin ratio, entered using the Microsoft Equation Editor 2.0.

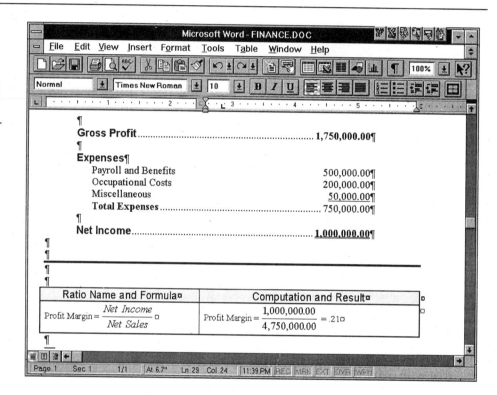

15. Save the document as RATIOS to the Advantage Diskette.

16. Close the document.

USING MICROSOFT GRAPH 5.0

The Microsoft Graph 5.0 mini-app is a full-featured charting application that helps you produce great-looking charts and graphs from within a Word document or PowerPoint presentation. Graph does not replace Excel, but it does provide a more convenient tool for embedding simple charts into documents. For example, you would use Graph to plot the values already stored in a Word table. If you had a situation that required further analysis of the figures, you would want to use Excel to perform the analysis and create the chart. In this section, we demonstrate how easy it is to add professional graphics to your work using Microsoft Graph 5.0.

Perform the following steps.

1. In Word, open the FAXNOTE document located on the Advantage Diskette. This fax provides a brief note with a table of research values. Your task in this section is to plot the values in a chart that will appear immediately below the table.

2. Move to the bottom of the document and position the insertion point inside the table.

3. To plot the values from a Word table, you must first select the table:
    CHOOSE: Table, Select Table
    The table should appear highlighted before proceeding.

4. There are two ways to load Microsoft Graph 5.0. You can insert a Graph object using the Insert, Object command or you can click the Insert Chart button (⬛) on the Standard toolbar in both Word and PowerPoint. Let's do it the easy way:
    CLICK: Insert Chart button (⬛)
    (*Note*: You can also create a chart from scratch. To do so, position the insertion point where you want the chart to appear and then click the Insert Chart button [⬛]. A Datasheet window appears where you enter the values that you want to plot. You can then proceed as illustrated in this exercise.)

5. Microsoft Graph 5.0 immediately goes to work analyzing the table. When it finishes loading, the ChartWizard appears, ready to lead you through the various formatting options. On the first page of the ChartWizard, you specify the chart type. By default, Graph displays the chart in a 3-D Column. To retain this chart type and continue:
    PRESS: (Enter) or CLICK: Next >

6. On the second page of the ChartWizard, you specify the format for the 3-D Column chart:
    SELECT: Option 4 (the default)
    PRESS: (Enter) or CLICK: Next >

7. On the third page, you have an opportunity to check the ChartWizard's selection of the data series to plot from the table. In this example, the ChartWizard has incorrectly identified the first row as a data series. Let's correct that assumption:
    SELECT: Category (X) Axis Labels option button in the Use first row for group
    PRESS: (Enter) or CLICK: Next >

8. On the fourth and final page of the ChartWizard, you can enter titles for the top line of the chart and for the axes. In the Axis Titles group, do the following:
    TYPE: Years into the Category (X) text box
    TYPE: Cases into the Value (Z) text box
    PRESS: (Enter) or CLICK: Finish command button
    The ChartWizard disappears, leaving the Datasheet window. Your screen should now appears similar to Figure 3.9.

Figure 3.9

The Datasheet and
Graph object.

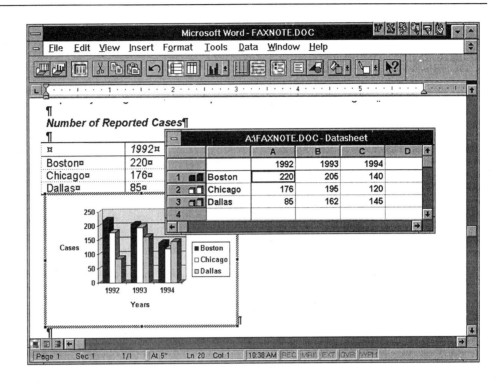

9. Since you are not going to edit the values in the table, remove the
    Datasheet window:
    CLICK: View Datasheet button (⊞) in the toolbar

    (*Note*: The process of formatting the chart in Microsoft Graph 5.0 is
    identical to how you would format a chart in Excel. To apply
    formatting, click the right mouse button on any item in the chart to
    display its shortcut menu. From this menu, choose the desired
    formatting command. Figure 3.10 provides a quick reference to the
    Graph toolbar buttons.)

Figure 3.10

The Graph toolbar.

10. Size the chart to the width of the table by dragging its handles.

11. To exit Microsoft Graph and return to the document:
    CLICK: in the document, outside of the chart frame

12. Position the insertion point to the left of the chart and press (**Enter**) to insert a blank line between the table and the chart object. (*Caution*: Do not press (**Enter**) if the chart appears selected with handles around its border. Be careful when you position the insertion point.)

13. To format the chart's border:
    RIGHT-CLICK: the mouse pointer anywhere on the chart
    CHOOSE: Borders and Shading
    SELECT: Shadow from the Preset Group
    PRESS: (**Enter**) or CLICK: OK

14. Save the document as FAXDONE to the Advantage Diskette. Your screen should now look similar to Figure 3.11.

Figure 3.11

The completed chart, created using Microsoft Graph 5.0.

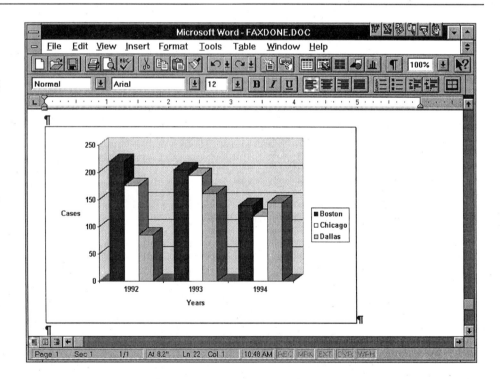

15. Let's assume that you made a mistake in entering Dallas' figures for 1992. The number in the Word table should read 185, not 85. Position the insertion point in the Word table and correct the value for Dallas.

16. Notice that the chart is not linked to the Word table. When you change a value in the table, there is no effect on the chart. To update the chart, you must enter the new value into the Datasheet window as well:
DOUBLE-CLICK: the chart object

17. If you cannot see the Datasheet window:
CLICK: View Datasheet button (▦) on the toolbar

18. SELECT: cell A3 (for Dallas in 1992)

19. TYPE: 185
PRESS: [Enter]
The chart is automatically refreshed to show the new value.

20. To complete the editing process:
CLICK: in the document, outside of the chart frame

21. Save the document as FAXDONE to the Advantage Diskette, replacing the existing version.

22. Close the document.

Quick Reference *Using Microsoft Graph 5.0*	1. SELECT: a Word table (or position the insertion point in the document)
	2. CHOOSE: Insert, Object and SELECT: Microsoft Graph 5.0, or CLICK: Insert Chart button (▦)
	3. Follow the step-by-step instructions of the ChartWizard and then click the Finish command button.
	4. CLICK: in the document to return to the client application

USING MICROSOFT ORGANIZATION CHART 1.0

Microsoft's Organization Chart 1.0 mini-app is a scaled-down version of Banner Blue Software's Org Plus for Windows that allows you to create organizational charts and other hierarchical diagrams. Most commonly, you create an organizational chart to include in a Word document, such as a report or internal memo, or a PowerPoint presentation. Similarly to working with graphics, apply the principles of simplicity, emphasis, and balance to creating **organizational charts**.

In this section, you create the following organizational chart:

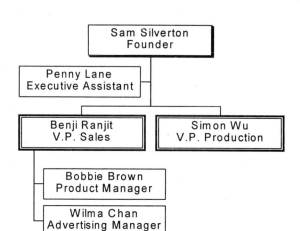

Perform the following steps.

1. In Word, open the PROMO document located on the Advantage Diskette. This letter is a promotional piece for Sam's Superior Sailboats, which is offering an opportunity to loyal customers who want to purchase seed stock. Your task is to create and embed an organizational chart showing Sam's management team.

2. Move to the end of the first paragraph and insert two blank lines. Position the insertion point as shown below:

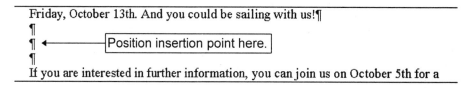

3. To create the organizational chart:
   CHOOSE: Insert, Object

4. In the Object dialog box:
   SELECT: Create New tab
   SELECT: Microsoft Organization Chart 1.0 from the Object Type list box
   PRESS: [Enter] or CLICK: OK
   The Organization Chart window appears as shown in Figure 3.12. Notice that the chart begins with only two levels: one box at the top level and three boxes directly underneath on the next level. Levels are also called **groups** in Organization Chart.

Figure 3.12

The Organization
Chart window.

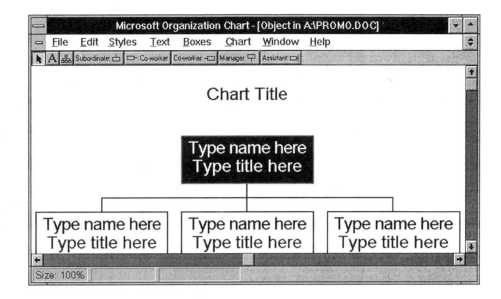

5. With the top box in the chart selected (as shown in Figure 3.12):
   TYPE: Sam Silverton
   PRESS: [Tab]
   TYPE: Founder
   Notice that the information you type automatically replaces the
   selected text in the box.

6. SELECT: lower left-hand box by clicking it once

7. Because we need only two branches under this organizational chart:
   PRESS: [Delete]
   The selected box is removed from the chart and the other two boxes on
   the same level re-align themselves under Sam Silverton's box.

8. SELECT: the left-hand box in the second level

9. TYPE: Benji Ranjit
   PRESS: [Tab]
   TYPE: V.P. Sales

10. SELECT: the right-hand box in the second level

11. TYPE: Simon Wu
    PRESS: [Tab]
    TYPE: V.P. Production

12. CLICK: on a blank area, inside the Organization Chart window, to remove the selection

13. To add a subordinate to Benji's team:
     CLICK: Subordinate button (Subordinate ☐) in the toolbar
     CLICK: Benji's box once
     You should see a new subordinate branch attach itself to Benji's box. Table 3.1 summarizes the buttons that are available in the toolbar for adding people to the chart.

Table 3.1	*Button*	*Description*
The Organization Chart's Toolbar	Subordinate: ☐	Adds a Subordinate below the selected box.
	☐ :Co-worker	Adds a Co-worker to the left of the selected box.
	Co-worker: ☐	Adds a Co-worker to the right of the selected box.
	Manager: ☐	Adds a Manager above the selected box.
	Assistant: ☐	Adds an Assistant beside the selected box.

14. To add another subordinate to Benji's box:
     CLICK: Subordinate button (Subordinate ☐) in the toolbar
     CLICK: Benji's box once again

15. To return the mouse pointer to an arrow and remove the highlighting:
     CLICK: Arrow button (▶) in the toolbar (if it is not already selected)
     CLICK: on a blank area, inside the Organization Chart window

16. To select an entire group or level of boxes:
CLICK: either subordinate box under Benji's box
CHOOSE: Edit, Select
CHOOSE: Group from the cascading menu
Notice that both boxes under Benji are now selected.

17. To change the style of a group of boxes:
CHOOSE: Styles from the menu
SELECT: the middle style on the first row (as shown at the right)

18. Enter the following two individuals into the boxes appearing beneath Benji Ranjit: Bobbie Brown, Product Manager and Wilma Chan, Advertising Manager.

19. Let's add an assistant for Sam Silverton:
CLICK: Assistant button (Assistant◻|)
CLICK: Sam Silverton's box
TYPE: Penny Lane
PRESS: Tab
TYPE: Executive Assistant

20. To make Sam Silverton's box stand out from the rest:
CLICK: Sam Silverton's box
CHOOSE: Boxes, Box Shadow
SELECT: any box shadow

21. To add a border to the two V.P.'s boxes:
CLICK: Benji Ranjit's box
PRESS: Ctrl+g as a shortcut to selecting all the boxes at the same level or group
CHOOSE: Boxes, Box Border
SELECT: any box border
(Hint: You can also press Ctrl+b to select an entire branch.)

22. To display more of the chart in the window:
CHOOSE: Chart, 50% of Actual

23. Let's return to the document:
CHOOSE: File, Exit and Return to A:\PROMO.DOC

24. When asked to Update the Object in A:\PROMO.DOC:
    PRESS: [Enter] or CLICK: Yes
    You are returned to the PROMO document and the organizational
    chart appears at the insertion point.

25. Position the mouse pointer over the organization chart and click once
    to select it for sizing.

26. DRAG: the sizing boxes to reduce the size of the chart
    Your document should now appear similar to Figure 3.13.

Figure 3.13

The completed
organizational
chart, created using
Organization Chart.

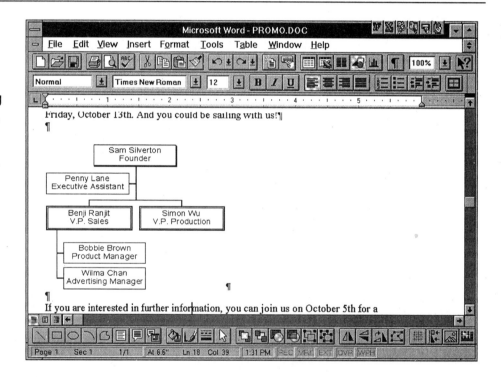

27. Save the document as ORGCHART to the Advantage Diskette.

28. Close the document.

Quick Reference *Using Microsoft* *Organization* *Chart 1.0*	1. Position the insertion point where you want to insert the object. 2. CHOOSE: Insert, Object 3. SELECT: Microsoft Organization Chart 1.0 on the Create New tab 4. PRESS: [Enter] or CLICK: OK 5. Edit and format the chart boxes. 6. CHOOSE: File, Exit and Return to *document*

USING MICROSOFT WORDART 2.0

The Microsoft WordArt 2.0 mini-app is an excellent tool for jazzing up standard documents. If you need to create company logos, newsletter headlines, or promotional pieces, WordArt can make your job easier and much more fun. Some examples of WordArt appear below:

WordArt can definitely help you to grab and keep the reader's attention. However, you should avoid inserting too many WordArt objects on the same page. Instead of enhancing your work, too many special effects can distract the reader.

Perform the following steps.

1. In Word, open the COMPUTER document located on the Advantage Diskette. You used this file previously to insert a graphic file and add a caption to a picture. Your task now is to insert a WordArt object in the heading of this flyer.

2. Notice that the heading is arranged into a two-cell table. In the left-hand cell, the title "Computer Corner" appears. You will place a WordArt object in the right-hand cell. Position the insertion point in the second or rightmost column of the table.

3. To create the heading using WordArt:
    CHOOSE: Insert, Object

4. In the Object dialog box:
    CLICK: Create New tab
    SELECT: Microsoft WordArt 2.0 from the Object Type list box
    PRESS: Enter or CLICK: OK
    The WordArt menu, toolbar, and Text Edit box (shown in Figure 3.14) assume control from Word's menu and toolbar.

Figure 3.14

Text Edit dialog box.

5. In WordArt's Text Edit box (also called the Enter Your Text Here box, for obvious reasons):
    TYPE: June 95

6. To see how the text will appear in your document:
    CLICK: Update Display command button
    The June 95 text appears in a frame, above the Text Edit box.

You can access most of WordArt's formatting features from its toolbar. The toolbar is divided into two sections. First, the drop-down menus allow you to apply a shape to the text, change the font style, and manipulate the font size. Second, the toolbar buttons provide access to most of the special effects for text, including stretching, rotating, and flipping text, and applying shadows, shading, and borders. All of these options are also available to be selected from the menu. The WordArt toolbar is labeled in Figure 3.15.

Figure 3.15

WordArt 2.0's
toolbar.

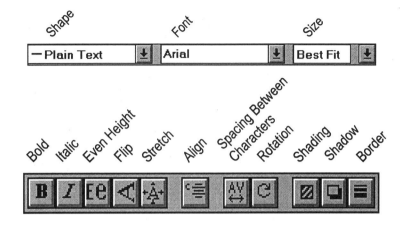

Let's apply some special effects to the June 95 heading:

1. To apply a shadow effect to the text:
    CLICK: Shadow button (▣)

2. From the drop-down list that appears:
    SELECT: the only "H" shadow shown in the list (at the bottom)

3. To ensure that the WordArt text fills the area that you've specified for
    the object:
    CLICK: Stretch button (▨)

4. From the Font drop-down menu:
    SELECT: Times New Roman

5. From the Shape drop-down menu:
    SELECT: Wave 1 (◣◢)

6. To return to the document:
    CLICK: in the document, outside of the WordArt frame

7. Size the WordArt object to match the display in Figure 3.16.

Figure 3.16

WordArt object after sizing.

8. Print the document.

9. Save the document as COMPUTER, replacing the existing version.

10. Close the document.

Quick Reference	1.	Position the insertion point where you want to insert the object.
Using Microsoft	2.	CHOOSE: Insert, Object
WordArt 2.0	3.	SELECT: Microsoft WordArt 2.0 on the Create New tab
	4.	TYPE: *the desired text* into the Text Edit box
	5.	SELECT: *the desired formatting options* from the toolbar and menu
	6.	CLICK: outside of the Text Edit box to return to the document

SUMMARY

This session let you practice inserting and editing objects using the Microsoft mini-apps, included with Microsoft Office. You used the ClipArt Gallery to find a logo for a company, Equation Editor to create a profit margin ratio, Graph to plot the values from a Word table,

Organization Chart to insert a management diagram into a document, and WordArt to spice up the heading of a flyer. Also in this session, you learned how to insert a graphic image file as a picture object.

Table 3.2 provides a list of the commands and procedures covered in this session.

Table 3.2	*Command*	*Description*
Command Summary	Insert, Object	Lets you create an object or insert an existing object into your document and access the Microsoft Office mini-apps.
	Insert, Picture	Lets you insert a graphic image that is stored as a file on the disk.
Graph	Insert Chart (▣)	Inserts a chart at the insertion point or creates a chart from an existing table of values.
	View Datasheet (▣)	Removes or displays the Datasheet of values to plot in a chart.
Organization Chart	Boxes, Box Shadow	Adds a shadow effect to a chart box.
	Boxes, Box Border	Adds a border to a chart box.
	File, Exit and Return	Leaves Organization Chart and updates your document.
WordArt	Shadow button (▣)	Applies a shadow effect to text.
	Stretch button (▣)	Forces the entered text to fill out the frame that borders the WordArt object.
	Font drop-down menu	Lets you select a font for the WordArt text object.
	Shape List drop-down menu	Lets you add special shape-effects to text, such as the Wave applied to the article heading.

KEY TERMS

clip art image   A computer graphic that you can insert into your document to make it more interesting or entertaining; the Microsoft ClipArt Gallery organizes clip art images for all Office applications.

graphic file   A computer graphic, created by an artist or scanned from an existing picture or photograph, that you can insert into your document using the Insert, Picture command.

groups   In Organization Chart, an entire horizontal level of co-workers.

mini-apps   Small application programs that are bundled with Microsoft Office to enhance the primary applications; most mini-apps are accessed using the Insert, Object command.

organizational charts   A diagram showing the internal management reporting structure of a company, organization, institution, or other such group; also used for flow chart diagrams.

palette   In Equation Editor, a list of additional options accessed through the toolbar for templates and symbols.

scanner   A hardware device that converts an existing picture or photograph into a computer image that is stored digitally on the disk.

symbol   In Equation Editor, a mathematical symbol (usually Greek) that is not available in the typical TrueType fonts provided by Windows.

template   In Equation Editor, a form or framework for entering mathematical elements, such as a fraction or square root.

EXERCISES

SHORT ANSWER

1. What is a mini-application? Name five mini-apps covered in this session.
2. How do mini-apps differ from the primary applications in Office?

3. What command is commonly used to insert objects from mini-apps?
4. How could you find out what mini-apps are available on your computer?
5. Name the Office applications that can access the ClipArt Gallery.
6. The Equation Editor's toolbar is divided into two areas. Explain.
7. How do you insert a space between variable names using the Equation Editor?
8. When would you want to use Excel to create a chart instead of using Microsoft Graph 5.0?
9. What term is used to describe organizational chart boxes that exist on the same level?
10. How would you correct a misspelled word in a WordArt object?

HANDS-ON

(*Note*: In the following exercises, save your documents onto and retrieve files from the Advantage Diskette.)

1. In the following exercise, you practice inserting objects from the Office mini-apps.
   a. Close all open documents.
   b. Load PowerPoint.
   c. Create a new PowerPoint presentation using the Blank Presentation option.
   d. SELECT: Title Slide AutoLayout option
   e. CLICK: "Click to add title" text on the new slide that appears
   f. TYPE: `Microsoft ClipArt Gallery 1.0`
   g. CLICK: "Click to add sub-title" text
   h. Insert a clip art image of your choice to the slide.
   i. CLICK: New Slide button on the Status bar
   j. SELECT: Graph AutoLayout option
   k. CLICK: "Click to add title" text
   l. TYPE: `Microsoft Graph 5.0`
   m. DOUBLE-CLICK: "Double click to add graph" text
   n. Create and format a new 3-D Column chart based on the following values, using Microsoft Graph 5.0:

	Actual	Budget
Widgets	120	125
Grapples	24	35
Grommets	88	90

   Your screen should appear similar to Figure 3.17.

Figure 3.17

Inserting a Graph
object into a
PowerPoint slide.

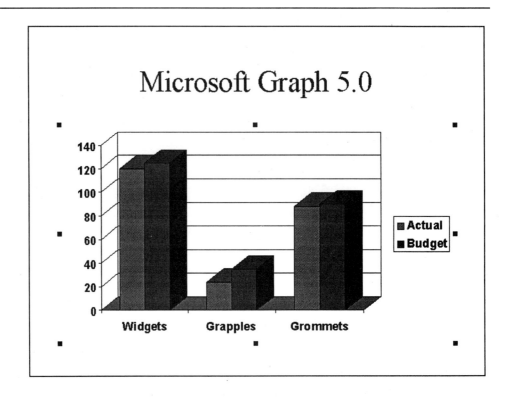

o. CLICK: New Slide button on the Status bar
p. SELECT: Org Chart AutoLayout option
q. CLICK: "Click to add title" text
r. TYPE: `Microsoft Organization Chart 1.0`
s. DOUBLE-CLICK: "Double click to add org chart" text
t. Insert the following organizational chart into the slide:

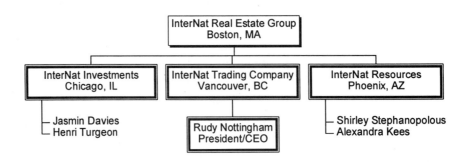

u. Save the PowerPoint presentation as MINIAPPS to the Advantage
   Diskette.
v. Quit PowerPoint.

2. Create a new document in Microsoft Word that presents ten different versions of the same WordArt object. Use the text "WordArt 2.0" and apply shape effects, fonts, and shadows. Once you've completed creating the objects, print the document and save it as ARTCLASS to the Advantage Diskette.

INTEGRATING MICROSOFT OFFICE VERSION 4.2/4.3: STEP-BY-STEP WITH OLE

Practice, Practice, Practice! Sound like an old gym coach you used to know? Well, we're probably emphasizing the same principles—essentially, practice makes perfect. In this session, you leave the "how to" of integrating Microsoft Office and work through a real-world example one object at a time. You'll experience the power of OLE first-hand in creating a newsletter using Microsoft Word. Okay people, time to get out on the field!

PREVIEW

When you have completed this session, you will be able to:

Insert and edit objects using WordArt.

•

Insert images from the ClipArt Gallery.

•

Insert graphic objects.

•

Create, edit, and format a hierarchical diagram using Organization Chart.

SESSION OUTLINE

Why This Session Is Important
Your Mission
Working with Text
Applying Special Effects to Text
Working with Graphics
Adding an Organizational Chart
Summary
Exercises

WHY THIS SESSION IS IMPORTANT

Whether you're an experienced computer user or a "newbie," application software programs can be difficult to learn. Have you ever noticed that there are always at least three ways to perform the same procedure? Well, we've noticed. That's one reason why we're giving you an opportunity to practice your new skills using real-world examples. In this session, you are led step-by-step through inserting and editing objects in a newsletter. Next session, you will prepare a departmental policy manual. Both of these exercises are designed to help you apply and integrate the primary components and mini-apps of Microsoft Office.

Here's the immediate situation: You are the communications manager for the Minestrone Soup Company. One of your duties at Minestrone is to create and disseminate a monthly employee newsletter. Your objective in this session is to finish next month's issue. Fortunately, the body of the newsletter has already been completed and only the front page requires some extra work. Having just completed a course on using Microsoft Office, you're ready to tackle the newsletter's cover page. Your personal objective is to add some flash and appeal to the cover.

In this session, you create a compound document using Microsoft Word. You also use Microsoft WordArt to apply special effects to text, Microsoft ClipArt Gallery to insert an image, Microsoft Organization Chart to create an organizational diagram, and the Insert Picture command to paste a scanned photograph into the document. The tasks in this session focus on embedding objects from the Microsoft Office mini-apps.

Before proceeding, make sure the following are true:

1. You have loaded the Microsoft Office Manager (MOM).
2. Your Advantage Diskette is inserted into drive A:.
3. You have loaded Microsoft Word 6.0 for Windows.

YOUR MISSION

Your mission is to create the following newsletter cover page for the Minestrone Soup Company. All of the necessary items are either included on the Advantage Diskette or must be created using the Office mini-apps. You may want to refer back to this page to clarify, or perhaps visualize, a section's objective.

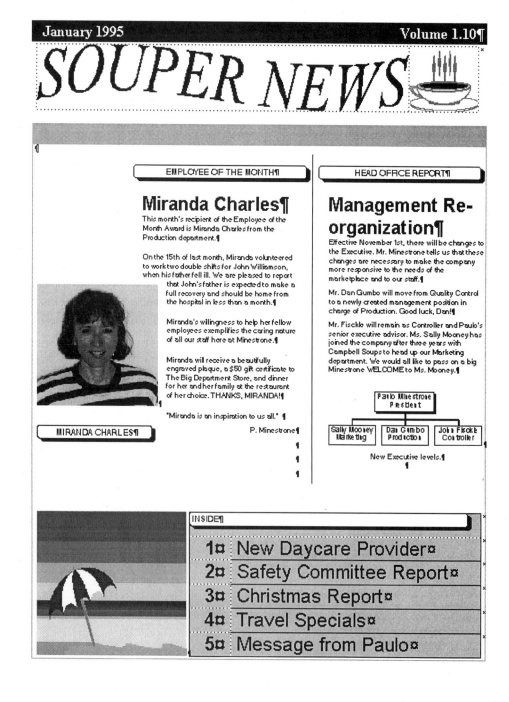

WORKING WITH TEXT

In this section, you retrieve the newsletter's cover page that was initially prepared by your assistants. Although they entered the body text for all the articles, you must create the headings and captions. To speed up the process, your thoughtful assistants have placed text boxes where the headings should be entered. This section provides an example of using text boxes and tables as placeholders in a Word document.

Perform the following steps.

1. Ensure that Microsoft Word 6.0 is loaded with its application window maximized.

2. Open the file named SOUPNEWS.DOC, located on the Advantage Diskette. This document automatically loads in Page Layout View. Your screen should appear similar to Figure 4.1.

Figure 4.1

The SOUPNEWS document file.

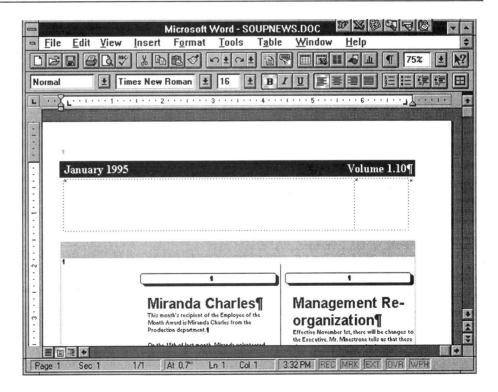

3. Position the mouse pointer over the text box that appears immediately above the article heading "Miranda Charles."

4. To position the insertion point in the text box:
   CLICK: left mouse button once
   You should see a flashing I-beam in the text box. (*Hint*: You can increase the display size of the document by choosing a zoom percentage from the Zoom Control drop-down menu in the toolbar.)

5. TYPE: employee of the month
   (*Note:* Thanks to your assistants and their use of formatting styles, the text is automatically formatted in uppercase as you type.)

6. Position the mouse pointer over the text box that appears immediately above the article heading "Management Reorganization" and click once to position the insertion point.

7. TYPE: head office report
   Again, the text is formatted in uppercase.

8. Scroll down the page using the mouse and scroll bars until you see a text box to the left of P. Minestrone's quotation for Miranda Charles. Position the mouse pointer over the text box and click once to position the insertion point.

9. TYPE: miranda charles

10. Scroll down further on the page until you see a table with the title "INSIDE." This table provides a quick glance of the topics contained in the newsletter. To enter the first topic in the table, position the insertion point in the second column of the first row. (*Hint:* You can always refer back to the sample cover page provided at the beginning of this session to clarify instructions.)

11. TYPE: New Daycare Provider
    PRESS: ⬇ once

12. TYPE: Safety Committee Report
    PRESS: ⬇ once

13. TYPE: Christmas Report
    PRESS: ⬇ once

14. TYPE: Travel Specials
    PRESS: ⬇ once

15. TYPE: `Message from Paulo`

16. Save the document as SOUPDONE onto the Advantage Diskette.

Great! You now have headings for the articles, a caption for the graphic of Miranda Charles, and a table of contents for this issue of the newsletter. Let's proceed to the next session where you will use Microsoft WordArt to draw and retain the reader's attention to your newsletter.

APPLYING SPECIAL EFFECTS TO TEXT

In this section, you create a WordArt object for the heading of the newsletter, SOUPER NEWS. Once inserted, you will then edit the heading to practice working with embedded objects. For more information on applying special effects to text, see the discussion in Session 3 on Using Microsoft WordArt 2.0.

Perform the following steps.

1. To begin, scroll the document window to view the top of the page.

2. Immediately below the date line, there is an outline for a two-column table. Position the insertion point in the first column of the table. (*Hint*: If selected properly, the table is surrounded by a hatched or shaded pattern.)

3. To create the heading using WordArt:
    CHOOSE: Insert, Object
    SELECT: Create New tab
    SELECT: Microsoft WordArt 2.0 from the Object Type list box
    PRESS: (Enter) or CLICK: OK
    The WordArt menu, toolbar, and Text Edit box appear.

4. In WordArt's Text Edit box:
    TYPE: SOUPER NEWS

5. To see how the text will appear in your document:
    CLICK: Update Display command button
    Your screen should now appear similar to Figure 4.2.

Figure 4.2

Inserting a
newsletter banner
using WordArt.

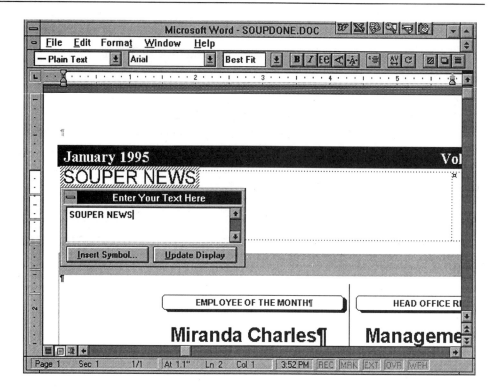

6. To insert the object and return to the Word document:
   CLICK: in the document, outside of the Text Edit box

7. The heading, SOUPER NEWS, now appears as a selected object in the table. Using the horizontal and vertical sizing handles, drag the object's borders to fit the entire area defined by the first column of the table. In other words, stretch the object to the right and downwards.

8. Let's add some spice to the heading to make it stand out from the other textual information on the page. Position the mouse pointer over the embedded WordArt object and do the following:
   DOUBLE-CLICK: the SOUPER NEWS WordArt object
   Notice that WordArt is launched and the text appears once again in the Text Edit box.

9. Using the WordArt toolbar buttons, add some special effects and formatting to the heading:
   CLICK: Stretch to Frame button (⊞)
   CLICK: Italic button (⊞)
   SELECT: Times New Roman from the Font drop-down list box
   SELECT: Wave 1 (◣◥) from the Shape drop-down list box

10. To return to the document:
    CLICK: in the document, outside of the Text Edit box
    Your document should now appear similar to Figure 4.3.

Figure 4.3

Applying special
effects to the
newsletter heading.

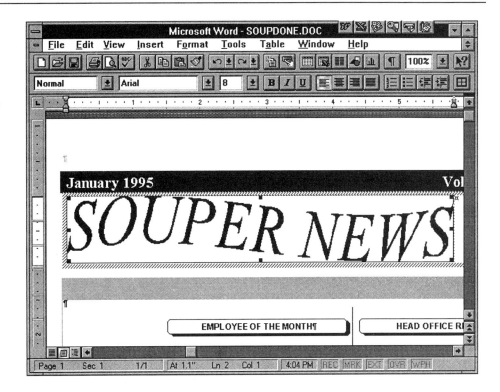

11. Save the document as SOUPDONE onto the Advantage Diskette,
    replacing the existing version.

WORKING WITH GRAPHICS

Newsletters seem to gain personality with the inclusion of graphics,
especially real-life photographs. In this session, you insert images from the
Microsoft ClipArt Gallery and from a photograph stored as a bitmap file
on the Advantage Diskette.

Back to the scenario: Several people in the company have told you that
they missed the last issue because it was "just another piece of paper in my
in-box." You now realize the importance of getting and keeping their
attention. To this end, you decide to peruse the ClipArt Gallery for a

catchy logo to use in addition to the SOUPER NEWS WordArt heading. You've also learned that Human Resources has photos of each employee. After some in-house searching and bartering, you were able to borrow Marketing's image scanner and save a picture of Miranda Charles onto the Advantage Diskette. You will place Miranda's photo on the cover of next month's newsletter. Let's get to work.

Perform the following steps to add a logo to the SOUPER NEWS heading.

1. To begin, scroll the document window to view the top of the page.

2. Immediately below the date line, position the insertion point in the second column of the table, to the right of the WordArt object "SOUPER NEWS."

3. To find a logo in the ClipArt Gallery:
    CHOOSE: Insert, Object
    SELECT: Create New tab
    SELECT: Microsoft ClipArt Gallery from the Object Type list box
    PRESS: [Enter] or CLICK: OK
    The ClipArt Gallery dialog box appears.

4. To limit the clip art images to those dealing with Household topics:
    SELECT: Household from the Category list box

5. In the second row of the thumbnail display:
    SELECT: Coffee Cup graphic (☕)
    PRESS: [Enter] or CLICK: OK
    The ClipArt Gallery is closed and you are immediately returned to Word and your newsletter.

6. Okay, who hid the graphic? Actually, the graphic has been inserted into the table, but needs to be sized to be seen. To resize the graphic, position the mouse pointer over the second column in the table and click the left mouse button once. You should see an outline of the graphic appear with sizing handles.

7. DRAG: the sizing handles to reduce the size of the graphic
    When you release the mouse button, you should see the coffee cup appear within the graphic's borders. (*Note*: You may have to drag the handles several times in order to reduce the graphic's size enough.)

8. Using the horizontal and vertical sizing handles, drag the graphic's borders to fit the entire area defined by the second column of the table. In other words, stretch or shrink the graphic to fit into the table.

9. Save the document as SOUPDONE onto the Advantage Diskette, replacing the existing version. Your screen should appear similar to Figure 4.4. (*Note*: Get into the habit of saving your work after each major addition or revision.)

Figure 4.4

Inserting clip art into a table on the newsletter.

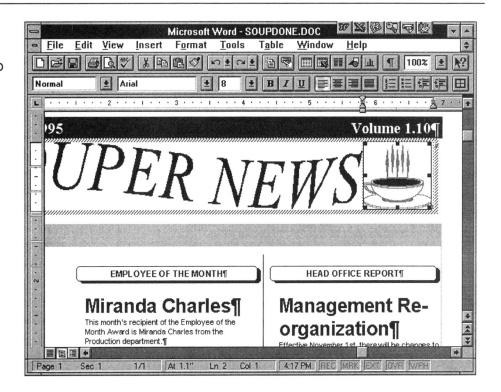

Perform the following steps to add a clip art image beside the Contents table.

1. To begin, scroll the document window to view the bottom of the page.

2. Fortunately for us, our assistants created a frame in Word to contain the graphic. To position the insertion point in the frame:
   CLICK: to the left of the Contents table, in the blank area
   You should see a hatched or shaded border appear around the area designated for the graphic.

3. To insert a clip art image into the frame:
   CHOOSE: Insert, Object
   SELECT: Create New tab
   SELECT: Microsoft ClipArt Gallery from the Object Type list box
   PRESS: [Enter] or CLICK: OK

4. To limit the clip art images to those dealing with backgrounds:
   SELECT: Backgrounds from the Category list box

5. Near the bottom of the thumbnail display for backgrounds, there is a beach scene with a red and white beach umbrella, called "At the Beach." Do the following:
   SELECT: At the Beach graphic (🏖)
   PRESS: [Enter] or CLICK: OK
   (*Hint:* The name of the graphic, At the Beach, appears below the thumbnail pictures in the dialog box.)

6. When you return to Word, the At the Beach scene is inserted into the document, spanning a large area at the bottom of the page. To resize the graphic, position the mouse pointer over the graphic and click the left mouse button once.

7. DRAG: the sizing handles to reduce the size of the graphic
   DRAG: the image itself to position the frame beside the Contents table

8. Using the horizontal and vertical sizing handles, drag the graphic's borders to fit neatly in the area left of the Contents table.

9. Save the document as SOUPDONE onto the Advantage Diskette, replacing the existing version. Your screen should appear similar to Figure 4.5.

Figure 4.5

Inserting clip art into a frame on the newsletter.

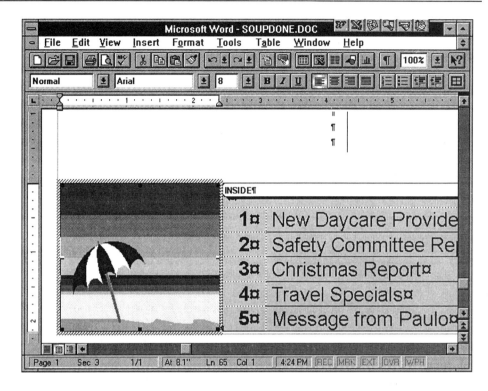

Perform the following steps to add a photograph to the newsletter.

1. To begin, scroll the document window to view the area above the caption for Miranda Charles and to the left of the article text.

2. Our assistants have placed another frame in the newsletter to hold the photograph. To position the insertion point in the frame:
    CLICK: above the "Miranda Charles" caption, in the blank area
    (*Caution:* Make sure that you are clicking above the caption and not above the article heading.) You should see a hatched border appear around the outline of the frame.

3. To insert a graphic file into the frame:
    CHOOSE: Insert, Picture
    SELECT: a: from the Drives drop-down list to access the files on the Advantage Diskette
    SELECT: All Graphic Files from the List Files of Type drop-down list
    SELECT: miranda.bmp from the File Name list box
    SELECT: Preview Picture check box
    (*Note:* Do not select the Link to File check box.) The Insert Picture dialog box should appear similar to Figure 4.6.

Figure 4.6

Previewing a
graphic file in the
Insert Picture
dialog box.

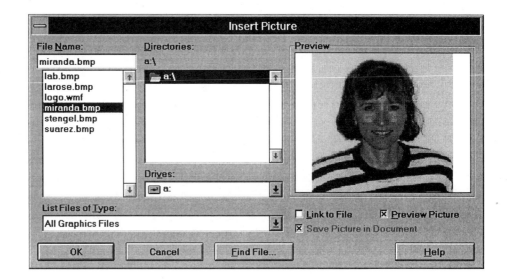

4. To insert the photograph into the newsletter:
   PRESS: [Enter] or CLICK: OK

5. If the photograph requires sizing in your document, drag the sizing
   handles to position the graphic as shown in Figure 4.7. (*Caution*: For
   obvious reasons, you should only drag the corner handles of
   photographs to ensure proportional sizing. Otherwise, your
   photographs will look like reflections in a circus mirror.)

Figure 4.7

Inserting a photograph into the newsletter.

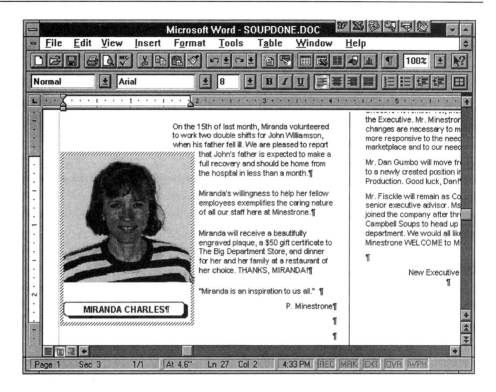

6. Save the document as SOUPDONE onto the Advantage Diskette, replacing the existing version.

ADDING AN ORGANIZATIONAL CHART

The president of Minestrone Soups, Paulo Minestrone himself, has asked that you emphasize the new executive personnel in your newsletter. In addition to running the front-page article entitled "Management Reorganization," you decide to insert an organizational chart depicting the new executive level. You ask your assistants to create a caption for the chart at the end of the article, and you then proceed with the following steps.

1. To begin, scroll the document window to view the article on Management Reorganization.

2. Immediately below the article text, there appears a blank line before the start of the caption "New Executive levels." Position the insertion point on this blank line, between the paragraph and the caption.

3. To create the organizational chart:
   CHOOSE: Insert, Object
   CLICK: Create New tab
   SELECT: Microsoft Organization Chart 1.0 from the Object Type list box
   PRESS: Enter or CLICK: OK

4. To edit the default text in the boxes of the sample chart:
   TYPE: Paulo Minestrone
   PRESS: Tab
   TYPE: President

5. Using the same procedure as above, click on each box to select it and then edit the text in the box. (*Hint*: Only click once on the box you want to select. If you click twice by mistake, the insertion point is placed in the box and you must then drag the I-beam mouse pointer across the text you want to replace.)

Leftmost Box	*Center Box*	*Rightmost Box*
Sally Mooney	Dan Gumbo	John Fisckle
Marketing	Production	Controller

6. When you are finished editing the chart:
   CHOOSE: File, Exit and Return to SOUPDONE.DOC

7. When you are asked to confirm that the object needs to be updated:
   PRESS: Enter or CLICK: Yes

8. Size the organizational chart to resemble the chart shown Figure 4.8.

Figure 4.8

Inserting an organizational chart into the newsletter.

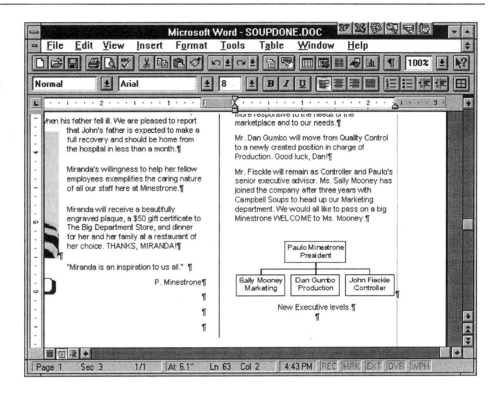

9. Now that you've finished creating the initial chart, let's go back and edit Mr. Minestrone's box to make it more distinctive. To begin:
DOUBLE-CLICK: the organizational chart object
After a few seconds, the chart appears in the Organization Chart window.

10. To enhance Mr. Minestrone's entry with a shadowed box:
CHOOSE: Boxes, Box Shadow
SELECT: *any of the shadow options that appear*

11. To return to the newsletter:
CHOOSE: File, Exit and Return to SOUPDONE.DOC

12. When you are asked to confirm that the object needs to be updated:
PRESS: Enter or CLICK: Yes
The new organizational chart sports a fancy shadowed box for Paulo Minestrone and plain boxes for the rest of the executive.

13. Save the document as SOUPDONE onto the Advantage Diskette, replacing the existing version.

14. Congratulations, you've completed the newsletter! Let's print it out to review our masterpiece:
CHOOSE: File, Print
PRESS: [Enter] or CLICK: OK

15. Compare the output from your printer with the sample page provided at the beginning of this session.

SUMMARY

This session led you step-by-step in creating a newsletter using Microsoft Word. Building a true compound document, you inserted a WordArt object, a clip art image, a photograph stored as a bitmap file, and an organizational chart. In addition, you used the Visual Editing feature of OLE to edit the objects once they were embedded into the document. (By the way, the president was so impressed that he personally authorized the purchase of a new computer for you to make the next issue even better!)

EXERCISES

(*Note*: In the following exercises, save your documents onto and retrieve files from the Advantage Diskette.)

1. In the following exercise, you select a new image from the Microsoft ClipArt Gallery to appear next to the Contents table.
   a. Load Microsoft Word and open the SOUPDONE document, stored on the Advantage Diskette.
   b. To begin, scroll the document window to view the clip art image called "At the Beach" appearing to the left of the Contents table.
   c. Position the mouse pointer over the object and click the right mouse button to display its context-sensitive shortcut menu.
   d. CHOOSE: Edit Microsoft ClipArt Gallery
   e. Let's choose a new clip art image:
      SELECT: People category
      SELECT: Crowd image, located at the bottom of the list box
   f. PRESS: [Enter] or CLICK: OK
   g. Size and position the new clip art image to match Figure 4.9.

Figure 4.9

Replacing a clip art image in the newsletter.

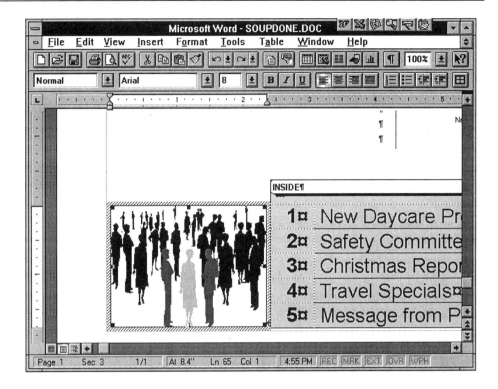

h. Save the document as SOUPDONE to the Advantage Diskette, replacing the existing version.
i. Print the revised newsletter.

2. Using Microsoft WordArt 2.0, change the heading from SOUPER NEWS to SOUP MONTHLY. Apply various special effects to the text using the WordArt Shape drop-down menu. Print the revised newsletter.

3. Using Microsoft Organization Chart 1.0, add Miranda Charles as an Administrative Assistant to Dan Gumbo in Production. Print the revised newsletter. Save the document as SOUPDONE to the Advantage Diskette, replacing the existing version.

SESSION 5

INTEGRATING MICROSOFT OFFICE VERSION 4.2/4.3: APPLYING WHAT YOU KNOW

Although presenting a complicated subject like OLE in a two-dimensional book is difficult, it doesn't compare to the challenges you face in assimilating and applying the material. Throughout this guide, you've been led step-by-step through exercises and examples. Anyone who can follow instructions can complete the first four sessions. Now we let the truly inspired students demonstrate their creativity and perseverance with a case study. Although there are no new concepts presented in this session, you will be surprised how much learning actually takes place!

PREVIEW

When you have completed this session, you will be able to:

Demonstrate your ability to work with and integrate multiple applications.

•

Demonstrate your ability to insert objects and pictures into a compound document.

Why This Session Is Important
Your Mission
Your First Step
Inserting Graphics
Inserting Sound Files
Inserting Tables and Charts
Adding an Organizational Chart
Take Five
Summary
Exercises

WHY THIS SESSION IS IMPORTANT

There are two fundamental stages in learning software: awareness and application. First, you must learn the capabilities of an application or software suite. Second, you learn how to apply the application's tools to perform specific tasks. The majority of computer training focuses on providing awareness (and rightly so—you can't perform a procedure if you don't know that it exists!) In this session, we assume that you've graduated beyond the awareness stage and want to learn how to apply what you already know.

This session is structured as a case study. You use the Microsoft Office applications and mini-apps to create a compound document. You will not find step-by-step instructions. In fact, the only instructions that you will receive are provided in the objective at the beginning of each section.

Before proceeding, make sure the following are true:

1. You have loaded the Microsoft Office Manager (MOM).
2. Your Advantage Diskette is inserted into drive A:.
3. You have loaded Microsoft Word 6.0.

YOUR MISSION

As the technology manager for the Human Resources division, your mission is to create an Online Employee Manual for the Minestrone Soup Company. For years now, the company has been disseminating its policy manuals in three-ring binders. To reduce its paper flow, Minestrone has decided to merge onto the information superhighway. Since each individual in the company has an electronic mail account, the president has asked you to prepare an Employee Manual that staff can access directly from their computer workstations.

Rather than starting from scratch, you've decided to edit the existing Employee Manual (written in Microsoft Word) and add some new features. Some of the new items must be created using the Microsoft Office mini-apps. Other items have been created by staff members and are provided on the Advantage Diskette. Table 5.1 provides a summary of the items you've received from other departments for inclusion in the manual.

Table 5.1	*File Name*	*Description*
Items to be added to the Online Employee Manual.	MANUAL.DOC	The existing Employee Manual, written using Microsoft Word 6.0 for Windows.
	LOGO.WMF	A graphic of the company logo in a Windows Metafile format, provided by Sally in Marketing.
	MESSAGE.WAV	A sound clip from Paulo Minestrone, the president, welcoming the employee to the new online manual.
	STENGEL.WAV	A sound clip about Margaret Stengel, the director of Human Resources.
	LAROSE.WAV	A sound clip about Robert LaRose, the manager responsible for Employee Assessments.
	SUAREZ.WAV	A sound clip about Maria Suarez, the manager responsible for Payroll and Benefits.
	STENGEL.BMP	A scanned photograph of Margaret Stengel.
	LAROSE.BMP	A scanned photograph of Robert LaRose.
	SUAREZ.BMP	A scanned photograph of Maria Suarez.
	SAFETY.XLS	An Excel worksheet detailing the company's safety record, supplied by Bob in Human Resources.

You will now create a living document that includes an audio greeting from the company president, the company logo, photos and sound bites from several key executives in the Human Resources division, and the company's safety record presented as a table and a chart. Now's the time to apply what you've learned!

YOUR FIRST STEP

Your objective for this section is to load the existing Employee Manual document into Microsoft Word. The document is stored as MANUAL.DOC on the Advantage Diskette. Figure 5.1 provides a thumbnail view of the four pages contained in the document. Review the pages and note the items contained in the curly braces {}. You will replace these items with the object specified in the braces.

Figure 5.1

Displaying pages from the MANUAL document using a thumbnail view.

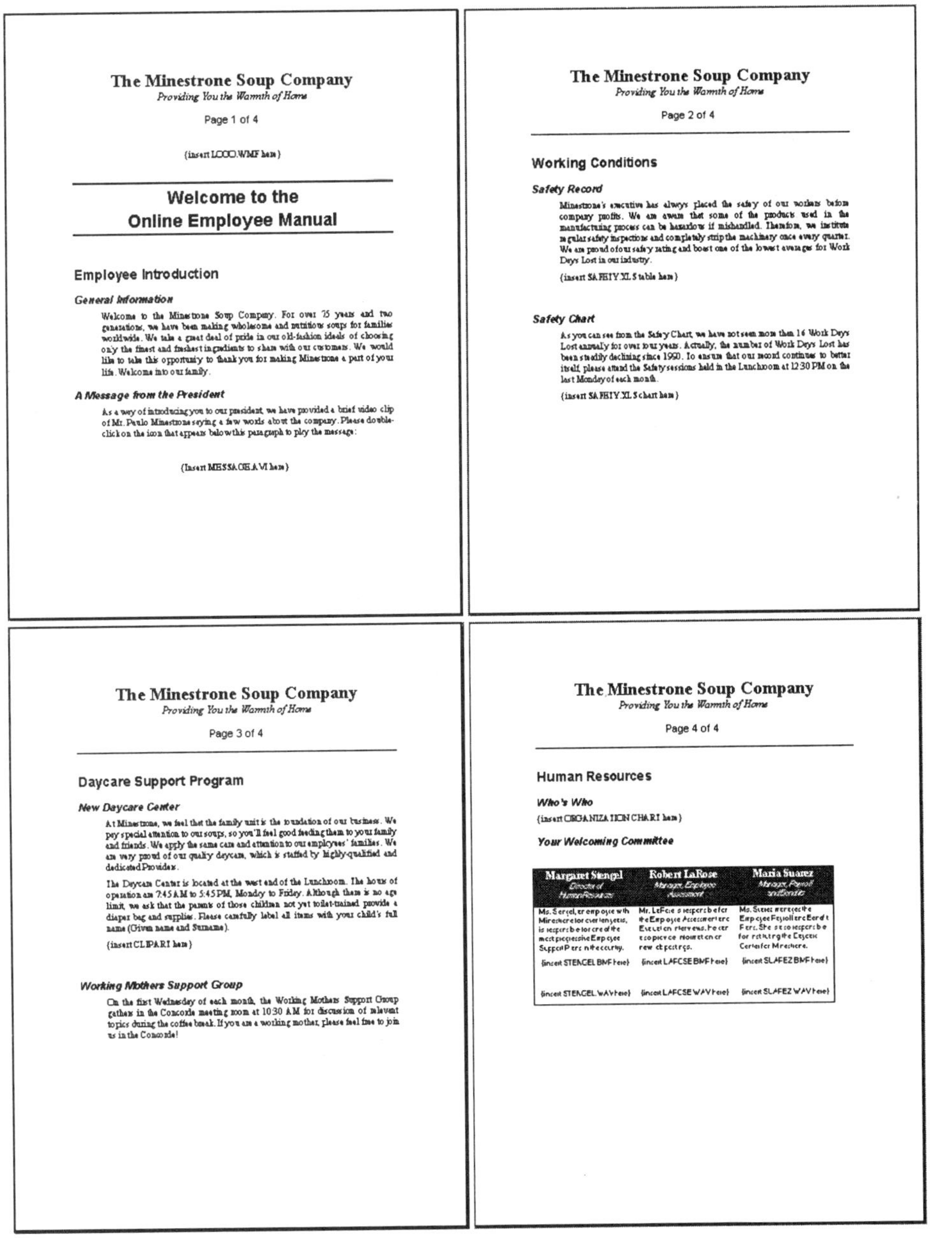
The Minestrone Soup Company
Providing You the Warmth of Home
Page 1 of 4
Welcome to the
Online Employee Manual
Employee Introduction
General Information
A Message from the President

The Minestrone Soup Company
Providing You the Warmth of Home
Page 2 of 4
Working Conditions
Safety Record
Safety Chart

The Minestrone Soup Company
Providing You the Warmth of Home
Page 3 of 4
Daycare Support Program
New Daycare Center
Working Mothers Support Group

The Minestrone Soup Company
Providing You the Warmth of Home
Page 4 of 4
Human Resources
Who's Who
Your Welcoming Committee
Margaret Stengel
Robert LaRose
Maria Suarez

INSERTING GRAPHICS

In this section, you embed graphics from the Microsoft ClipArt Gallery and from graphic files stored on the Advantage Diskette. You will have to size the graphics once they've been inserted into the document. Make sure that you delete the text in the curly braces when you insert the graphics.

Perform the following steps.

1. Move to the top of Page 1.

2. Delete the text "{insert LOGO.WMF here}."

3. Insert the LOGO.WMF file, which is stored on the Advantage Diskette, as shown in Figure 5.2. Size the logo so that Page 1 does not run onto Page 2. (*Note*: Do not link the picture with the file on the disk.)

Figure 5.2

Inserting the
LOGO.WMF file.

4. To ensure that there is enough disk space to save this document, you should place it on your hard disk. Save the document as MANUAL1.DOC to the hard disk directory of your choice.

5. Move to Page 3.

6. Replace the text "{insert CLIPART here}" with the ClipArt image that appears in Figure 5.3. Resize the image to prevent an extra page break from occurring.

Figure 5.3

Inserting an image from the ClipArt Gallery.

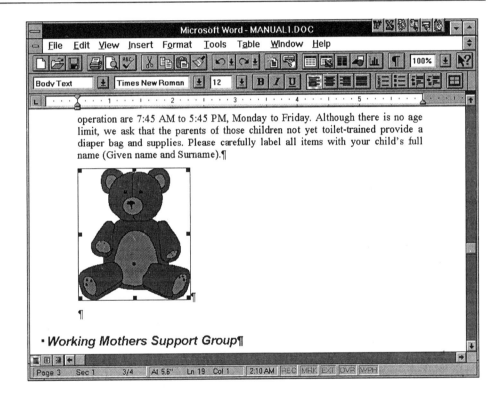

7. Move to Page 4.

8. In the table, replace the text "{insert *NAME*.BMP here}" with the correct graphic images stored on the Advantage Diskette. After sizing each of the graphic images, your screen should appear similar to Figure 5.4. (*Note*: Do not link the pictures to the files on the disk.)

Figure 5.4

Inserting scanned
photographs.

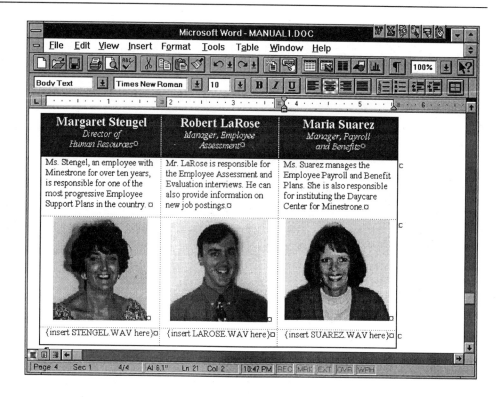

9. Save your work as MANUAL1.DOC to the hard disk.

INSERTING SOUND FILES

You insert sound objects into a document using the same steps that you
have learned for inserting graphic files. However, only computers that
meet the MPC (Multimedia PC) hardware specification will be able to
play the audio clips stored on the Advantage Diskette. If you experience
problems inserting or playing these sound files, skip to the next section.

Perform the following steps:

1. Move to the bottom of Page 1.

2. Delete the text "{insert MESSAGE.WAV here}."

3. Create an object in the document that links to the MESSAGE.WAV
    file stored on the Advantage Diskette. (*Hint:* You create an object from
    an existing file and then display the object as an icon in your

document.) Before proceeding, ensure that Page 1 does not run onto Page 2. When you have finished inserting the audio clip, your screen should appear similar to Figure 5.5.

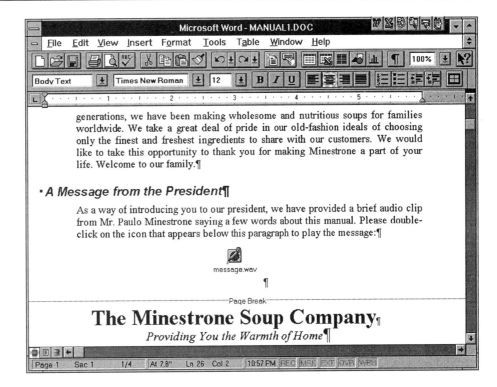

Figure 5.5

Linking to a greeting message from the President.

4. Save your work as MANUAL1.DOC to the hard disk.

5. To play the WAV audio clip:
DOUBLE-CLICK: message.wav icon (🖉)
If your computer can play WAV files, the clip begins to play.

Now, you need to insert the audio clips for each person in the Human Resources division.

1. Move to the table on Page 4.

2. Replace the text "{insert *NAME*.WAV here}" with the correct sound files stored on the Advantage Diskette. (*Hint:* You create an object from an existing file and then display the object as an icon in your document. Do not establish a link to the file.) Your screen should appear similar but not identical to Figure 5.6.

Figure 5.6

Inserting WAV
audio files.

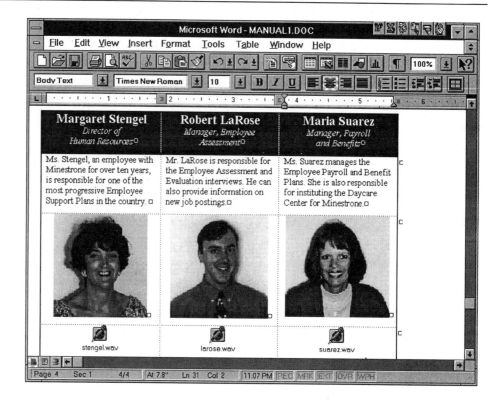

3. Play each of these audio clips.

4. Save your work as MANUAL1.DOC to the hard disk.

INSERTING AN EXCEL TABLE AND CHART

Now we'll add some hard figures to the Employee Manual document. In this section, you embed the SAFETY.XLS worksheet information into the Employee Manual document. The worksheet file is stored on the Advantage Diskette.

Perform the following steps.

1. Move to Page 2.

2. Delete the text "{insert SAFETY.XLS table here}."

3. With the insertion point on the same line where you deleted the text, insert the table from the SAFETY.XLS file. (*Hint*: Remember to use the Create from File tab, but do not select the Link to File option.) Your screen should now appear similar to Figure 5.7.

Figure 5.7

Embedding an Excel table into the document.

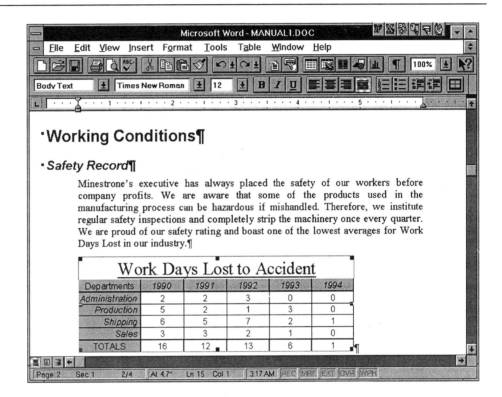

4. Delete the text "{insert SAFETY.XLS chart here}."

5. Open the SAFETY.XLS worksheet and then drag and drop the chart from the second workbook page into the MANUAL document.

6. You will have to remove all the blank lines on the page and size the chart to ensure that all the information fits on a single page. Your screen should appear similar to Figure 5.8 when you are finished.

Figure 5.8

Embedding an Excel chart into the document.

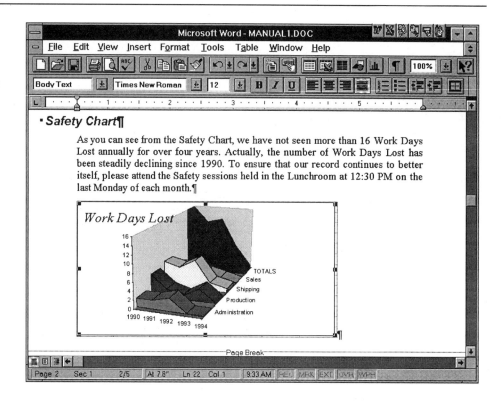

7. Save your work as MANUAL1.DOC to the hard disk.

ADDING AN ORGANIZATIONAL CHART

To provide a visual representation of the management structure in the Human Resources division, you've decided to add an organizational chart of the three top-level managers. Use the following sample as a guide for creating your own chart:

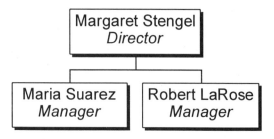

Perform the following steps.

1. Move to the top of Page 4.

2. Delete the text "{insert ORGANIZATION CHART here}."

3. With the insertion point on the same line where you deleted the text, add a new organizational chart like the one that appears above. Your screen should appear similar to Figure 5.9. Again, you must be careful not to make the chart too big since you want the information to be displayed on a single page.

Figure 5.9

Inserting an organizational chart.

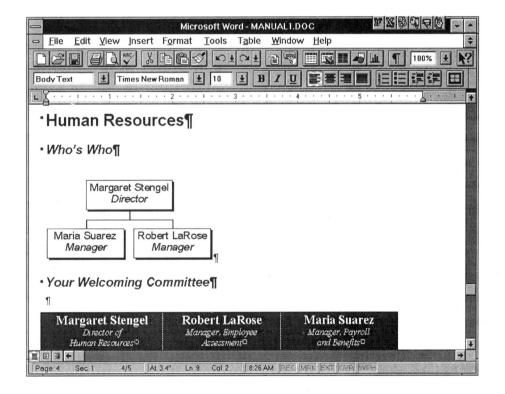

4. Save your work as MANUAL1.DOC to the hard disk.

5. Print the document and then compare it to the thumbnail view in Figure 5.10. (*Note*: Some printers may not be able to reproduce the graphics to match their display quality on your computer's monitor.)

Figure 5.10

The finished
product!

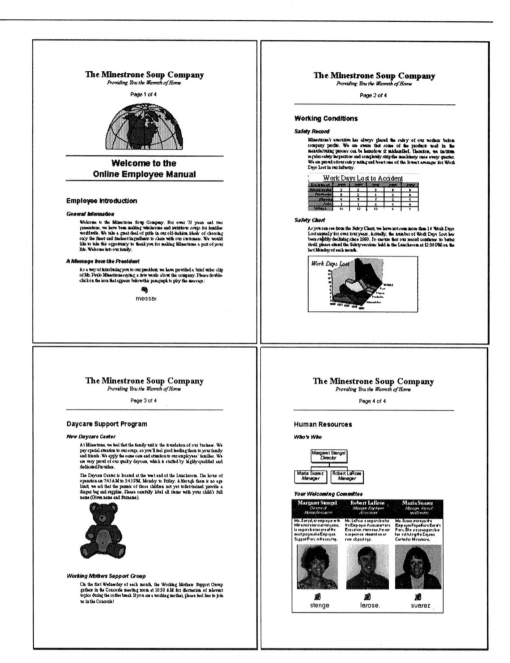

TAKE FIVE

The president has just come into your office and asked you to make an
impromptu presentation on the Online Employee Manual project to the
executive committee. You have ten minutes to prepare for the presentation
and get to the meeting. Fortunately, you remember that the boardroom has
a computer with Microsoft Office and a large display screen. You've used

it many times in the past to display PowerPoint presentations for training seminars. Take five minutes to turn the Online Employee Manual into an impressive PowerPoint presentation. Ready, Set, and Go!

Figure 5.11 shows one example of a PowerPoint slide created from the Online Employee Manual. Make sure that you save your work before proceeding.

Figure 5.11

Creating a PowerPoint slide presentation from the Online Employee Manual.

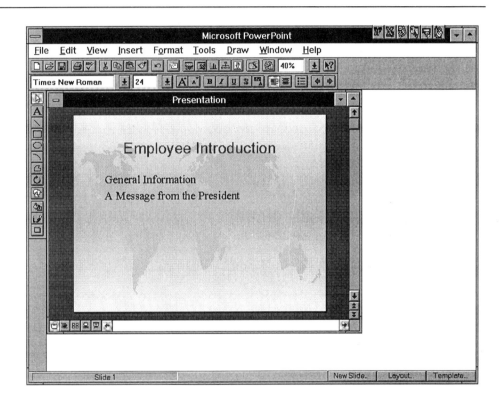

SUMMARY

This session provided you with an opportunity to test your knowledge in using and integrating Microsoft Office. Starting with a basic Microsoft Word document, you inserted and manipulated clip art images, scanned photographs, sound bites, an Excel table and chart, and an organizational chart. After completing the document, you created a slide show presentation outlining its major topics.

Congratulations on completing this guide. We hope that you can begin applying this knowledge in your work or school projects immediately. Good luck with Microsoft Office!

EXERCISES

(*Note*: In the following exercises, save your documents onto and retrieve files from the Advantage Diskette.)

1. In the following exercise, you select a new clip art image for the company logo.
   a. Move to the top of Page 1.
   b. Select the LOGO.WMF object that you inserted into the document at the beginning of this session.
   c. Using the Clip Art Gallery, select a new object for the company logo and then size it accordingly. Figure 5.12 shows one example of a new logo.

Figure 5.12

Inserting a new image for the company logo.

    d. Move to Page 3.

    e. Replace the Teddy Bear clip art image with a new image from the Clip Art Gallery.

    f. Save the document as MANUAL2.DOC to your hard disk.

2. You've just received a call from Bob in the Human Resources division. It seems that the SAFETY.XLS spreadsheet file that he had given you contained some incorrect information. Edit and update the table and chart on Page 2 using the new information shown below:

Work Days Lost to Accident					
Departments	1990	1991	1992	1993	1994
Administration	4	1	1	0	1
Production	5	2	3	3	0
Shipping	6	5	7	2	1
Sales	3	3	2	1	0
TOTALS	18	11	13	6	2

INTEGRATING MICROSOFT OFFICE VERSION 4.2/4.3